Google AppSheet
Advanced

⁝

Advanced App Building

By Daniel Melehi
Updated April 2025 Edition

©2025

Contents

3

5

Introduction

Welcome to *Google AppSheet Advanced: Advanced App Building*, a comprehensive guide crafted specifically for those seeking to push their AppSheet skills beyond the basics. This book delves into a wide array of advanced features and techniques, designed to help you build highly customizable, performance-driven applications. Whether you're already familiar with the fundamentals of AppSheet or have gained experience building simpler apps, you will find new possibilities and in-depth strategies to continually refine your solutions.

Throughout the chapters, we'll focus on robust data structures, performance optimization, and strategic workflows that fit complex business requirements. We'll also explore integration with external services, advanced calculations, user access management, and ways to future-proof your projects. Each chapter is filled with insightful examples and best practices, enabling you to build applications that not only function effectively but also offer a professional user experience.

Key elements of this book include:

- Real-world examples illustrating advanced data relationships, automated workflows, and security configurations.
- Practical tips on integrating with external APIs, collaborating with teams, and creating dynamic user interfaces.
- A guide to advanced troubleshooting and performance optimization, so you can keep your apps running smoothly.

By the end of this book, you'll be well-equipped with the knowledge and best practices needed to orchestrate powerful, secure, and scalable AppSheet implementations. We invite you to dive in and explore each chapter, applying the insights to your unique projects and discovering novel methods to extend AppSheet's capabilities.

Chapter 1: Designing Complex Data Structures

Building advanced, scalable applications hinges on well-thought-out data structures. In AppSheet, this means going beyond simple tables and embracing techniques that ensure data integrity, reduce redundancy, and deliver efficient performance. Let's explore how to craft complex data structures that can adapt to change, handle varied data sources, and support the sophisticated functionality demanded by modern business scenarios.

UNDERSTANDING THE VALUE OF STRUCTURED DATA

A crucial step in developing more advanced apps is recognizing that thoughtfully organized data leads to manageable and efficient solutions. Whether you're dealing with multiple teams, connected workflows, or evolving requirements, a strong data foundation sets the stage for consistent growth. By keeping tables structured and well-defined, you'll save time on future enhancements and simplify troubleshooting.

STRATEGIC APPROACHES TO NORMALIZATION

Data normalization is about eliminating duplicate information and organizing data in a way that minimizes redundancy. In AppSheet, this often starts with identifying which fields belong in which tables. Consider these guidelines for building normalized data models:

- **One Purpose per Table** – Group related attributes together under a clear purpose, ensuring each table addresses a unique aspect of the data.
- **Limited Repetition** – If you find the same data repeated across multiple tables, abstract it into a dedicated table with references to avoid data duplication.
- **Consistent Naming Conventions** – Creating uniform names for columns and tables reduces confusion when referencing data in expressions.

LEVERAGING COMPLEX KEYS

Keys are the backbone of any well-organized database. In AppSheet, you'll often use keys to reference rows across tables, powering relationships and facilitating seamless navigation. While a simple primary key might suffice in basic apps, advanced scenarios may require composite keys or carefully formatted unique IDs:

- **Composite Keys** – Combine multiple columns to form a key, especially when a single field doesn't adequately represent entity uniqueness (e.g., *OrderID + ProductID*).
- **AppSheet-Generated GUIDs** – Use *UNIQUEID()* or *RANDBETWEEN()* expressions to ensure system-wide

uniqueness of keys, helping avoid collisions and manual errors.

PLANNING FOR MULTIPLE DATA SOURCES

Advanced AppSheet applications often pull data from diverse platforms—spreadsheets, SQL databases, cloud storage, or third-party APIs. To manage complexity efficiently, keep these principles in mind:

1. **Centralized Data Management** – Determine a central 'source of truth.' Any secondary data sources should feed into or from this primary location, ensuring consistent updates.
2. **Schema Alignment** – Make sure columns and data types align across sources to prevent conflicts when establishing references or performing calculations.
3. **Data Refresh Strategy** – Decide how often data should synchronize. Real-time updates may be unnecessary for certain tasks, while others demand frequent or instantaneous data checking.

ENFORCING DATA INTEGRITY

As your data structures grow more complex, maintaining their integrity becomes increasingly important. Implement validation rules, reference actions, and conditional forms to lock in accurate, high-quality data. Consider setting up:

- **Required Fields** – Mark critical fields as required to ensure essential information is always collected.
- **Enum Constraints** – Limit possible values for given columns, reducing errors or invalid entries.

- **Reference Integrity** – Configure "IsPartOf" relationships and other references in a way that enforces the proper deletion or update cascades when related data changes.

OPTIMIZING FOR SCALABILITY

Scalability is crucial when designing advanced data structures. As your application grows, you'll want to ensure that queries remain fast, and that users can reliably interact with your app without performance bottlenecks. Key strategies here include:

- **Partitioning Large Data Sets** – Split massive tables into logical sections or leverage security filters that load only necessary data for each user.
- **Strategic Indexing** – In connected SQL databases, index commonly queried columns to speed up data retrieval.
- **Reducing Latency with Precomputed Values** – When dealing with repetitive calculations, consider using virtual columns that store results for quicker display, or materialize data in dedicated tables when performance truly needs optimization.

VISUAL OVERVIEW: A SAMPLE DATA ARCHITECTURE

Table Name	Primary Purpose	Key Column	References

Users	Stores user profile details and roles	UserID	-
Projects	Maintains project info and ownership	ProjectID	UserID (to *Users*)
Tasks	Contains individual tasks and metadata	TaskID	ProjectID (to *Projects*)

In this simplified setup, we see distinct tables with clear key columns and logical references. Consider more complex relationships (many-to-many, nested sub-tables) and data constraints when your app demands detailed dependency tracking.

CONCLUSION

Mastering complex data structures is an essential step toward developing high-performance AppSheet applications. By normalizing data, carefully managing keys, and enforcing strong integrity rules, you can produce agile, reliable solutions that scale seamlessly as your projects evolve. Up next, we'll explore how to maximize these structures using advanced table references that further enhance the interactivity of your AppSheet apps.

Chapter 2: Advanced Table Relationships and References

In robust AppSheet applications, complex relationships between tables are key to delivering seamless data flow and a smooth user experience. By using advanced references and schema designs, you can connect records across multiple tables, empower data integrity controls, and create highly interactive forms. This chapter dives deep into the intricacies of creating and managing intricate table relationships, helping you make the most of AppSheet's data-linked capabilities.

REFINING ONE-TO-MANY RELATIONSHIPS

A foundational structure for many apps is the one-to-many relationship—one record in a parent table linking to several child records in another table. While the concept is straightforward, AppSheet provides numerous tools to polish the user experience and enforce data consistency:

- **Inline Child Views** – Present child records directly within a parent detail view for quick reference and editing.
- **Automatic Child Form Creation** – Enable "IsPartOf" to tie child tables to parent tables, letting you automatically add child records from within the parent form.
- **Reference Actions** – Configure custom actions in the parent table to create, update, or delete child records in bulk, fostering efficient data maintenance.

MANAGING MANY-TO-MANY RELATIONSHIPS

If you need to associate multiple records in one table with multiple records in another, a many-to-many structure is essential. In AppSheet, the typical approach is to introduce a bridging table, sometimes called a "join table." This intermediary layer tracks relationships between two (or more) entities by storing their respective keys:

- **Join Table Structure** – Create a new table featuring reference columns pointing to each primary table (e.g., *Projects* and *Tasks*), ensuring data integrity via key constraints.
- **Inline Forms on the Join Table** – Embed a form within each parent record, making it simple to add associations to the linked table.
- **Efficient Filtering** – Build slices or leverage expressions in your join table to display only relevant cross-linked records, optimizing large-scale data navigation.

UTILIZING REVERSE REFERENCES

Reverse references provide an automatic way to see which child rows point to a specific parent row. While standard references let one table recognize its parent, reverse references display child information within the parent. This bidirectional approach opens up possibilities like inline child views and dynamic forms:

- **Streamlined Navigation** – Users can jump directly between children and parent rows without having to manually locate related data.
- **Comprehensive Dashboards** – Combine parent details and reverse-referenced lists in one place to build a holistic record summary.
- **Conditional Logic** – Use expressions that check child rows in real time (e.g., *COUNT([Related Child Records])* to dynamically activate certain features or forms in the parent record.

NESTED REFERENCES AND HIERARCHICAL DATA

Some projects benefit from layered data, where a parent table references a child table, which itself references another table, and so on. With careful design, you can create a logical chain of references that keeps data synchronized while allowing for powerful drill-down views:

- **Layered "IsPartOf" Chains** – Attach each subsequent child to its parent using the "IsPartOf" setting, enabling automatic cascading of records when they are added or removed.
- **Multi-Level Navigation** – Configure views that traverse multiple levels of data, helping users move smoothly from overarching categories to specific details.
- **Consolidated Actions** – Group actions that trigger changes on multiple layers of referenced records, minimizing repetitive tasks and user input.

ENHANCING REFERENCES WITH VIRTUAL COLUMNS

Virtual columns are perfect for calculating derived values across references, often delivering insights drawn from linked data. By referencing multiple tables in an expression, you can build context-aware fields that boost user awareness and drive key operations:

- **Summary Calculations** – Aggregate totals or averages from child rows, displaying meaningful metrics in parent records (e.g., total task hours for a given project).
- **Cross-Table Lookups** – Pull in data from related tables using syntax like *[ReferencedRow].[SomeField]*, eliminating repetitive references in the UI.
- **Conditional Triggers** – Combine virtual columns with workflows to kick off actions only when certain conditions involving linked tables are met.

BEST PRACTICES FOR CONSISTENT RELATIONSHIPS

When building advanced references, a few core principles will keep your data accurate and your workflows efficient:

Technique	Description
Reuse System-Generated Key Columns	AppSheet's default keys minimize duplication and collisions, which is especially useful in complex references.

Monitor Behaviors	**Delete**	Set up cascading deletes or block removals if child records exist, preventing orphaned rows and data inconsistencies.
Apply Column Naming	**Clear**	Use transparent column names (e.g., *CustomerID_Ref*) to avoid confusion when referencing or building formulas.

By committing to these guidelines, your relationships will stay organized, and your references will scale effectively as your application grows. Whether you're establishing one-to-many links or orchestrating a multi-table data network, these advanced techniques ensure your AppSheet project remains flexible and easy to maintain.

CONCLUSION

Advanced table relationships and references power the central engine of well-structured AppSheet applications. By building many-to-many relationships, reverse references, and nested structures, you can unlock dynamic user journeys and seamless data synchronization. In the chapters ahead, you'll continue to refine these reference strategies, blending them with complex expressions, security measures, and performance optimizations that propel your apps to the next level.

Chapter 3: Dynamic Expressions and Conditional Workflows

In this chapter, we'll dive into advanced ways of using expressions and workflows in AppSheet to create dynamic, responsive applications. By crafting precise logic and leveraging condition-based triggers, you can automate complex scenarios, guide users toward relevant actions, and ensure that data remains accurate at all stages of your app's lifecycle. Let's explore how to harness these tools to build more interactive and robust solutions.

EXPANDING THE POWER OF EXPRESSIONS

Expressions are at the heart of your app's responsiveness. Whether you're validating inputs, calculating summaries, or showing/hiding UI elements, AppSheet expressions can adapt to various user actions and data updates. Moving beyond the basics involves thoughtfully combining multiple expressions, integrating references to other tables, and using conditional statements to tailor user experiences.

- **Combining Operators** – Blend arithmetic ($+$, $*$), logical (*AND*, *OR*), and comparison ($<$, $>$) operators in a single expression to construct more advanced scenarios.
- **Nested Expressions** – Layer *IF()*, *SWITCH()*, or *IFS()* statements to manage multi-step, condition-based logic. This helps you handle complexities such as nested validations or tiered workflows.
- **Referencing Related Records** – Pull data from other tables dynamically by referencing child or parent rows,

then combine that data with your current row's values to power decision-making.

OPTIMIZING USER INTERACTION WITH CONTEXT-AWARE FIELDS

A hallmark of advanced apps is the ability to adapt form fields, views, and menus based on the current user or role. By embedding expressions in column constraints or visibility settings, you can produce customized experiences for each situation:

- **Dynamic Show_If** – Hide or display fields contingent on user input or existing data. For example, show a shipping address field only if the user chooses a "Delivery Required" option.
- **Context-Based Valid_If** – Limit available choices in a dropdown list according to another column's value or the user's role, reducing input errors and ensuring data relevance.
- **Conditional Formatting** – Color-code rows or highlight key values when certain thresholds are met (e.g., overdue tasks, flagged incidents), simplifying at-a-glance recognition.

LEVERAGING CONDITIONAL WORKFLOWS

Workflows automate routine tasks—like emailing a manager or updating a record—whenever specific events happen. By layering conditional logic, each workflow can target precisely the right conditions to trigger an action. This way, you avoid unnecessary notifications and keep your data processes streamlined.

1. **Event-Driven Triggers** – Define whether the workflow should activate on adds, updates, or deletes. Use expressions to narrow down the trigger even further, ensuring the workflow runs only under certain conditions.
2. **Post-Update Actions** – Automatically adjust child records or send confirmation messages once an update meets predetermined requirements. For instance, finalize a project's status when all tasks reach a "Complete" state.
3. **Multi-Step Chaining** – Sequence multiple actions within a single workflow. You could generate a PDF, email it to relevant stakeholders, and then flag a column in your table to confirm successful dispatch—all in one flow.

DYNAMIC EMAIL AND NOTIFICATION TEMPLATES

Conditional workflows often involve sending notifications. With expression-driven customization, you can tailor messages to the content and context:

- **Conditional Recipients** – Use *IF()* conditions to specify different recipients for various scenarios (e.g., operational alerts go to the service team, billing issues go to accounting).
- **Personalized Subjects and Bodies** – Insert expressions directly into templates to include user names, record details, or time-sensitive data in your subject line and message body.
- **Dynamic Attachments** – Generate documents, images, or spreadsheets on the fly based on new or updated data, letting recipients see the precise information they need to act upon.

COMBINING EXPRESSIONS WITH BOTS

Beyond basic workflows, AppSheet's automation features let you design Bots that wrap multiple processes into a single entity. You can fine-tune triggers, refine steps, and incorporate flexible branching:

- **Branching Logic** – Build conditional paths within a Bot, so different events or data criteria can trigger separate sets of actions, all within one overarching automation.
- **Scheduled Recurrence** – Combine time-based triggers with expression-based filters to run nightly or weekly checks, sending out alerts only if specified conditions are met.
- **Error-Recovery Sequences** – Design fallback actions that respond to specific failures, like re-sending notifications if an initial attempt doesn't succeed due to connectivity issues.

ADVANCED DEBUGGING TECHNIQUES

As expressions grow more complex, debugging becomes crucial. AppSheet provides an Expression Assistant and a Test feature to validate results step-by-step:

Tool	Function

Expression Assistant	Highlights syntax errors and suggests possible corrections or relevant columns, ensuring you keep your expressions precise.
Test Function	Allows you to input sample values and see the resulting output of an expression before finalizing it in your app.

Employ these tools to troubleshoot any unexpected outcomes or performance hiccups, ensuring that your workflows fire only when desired and your expressions always deliver correct results.

BEST PRACTICES FOR RELIABILITY AND MAINTAINABILITY

Working with dynamic expressions and conditional workflows can significantly enhance your app's complexity. Safeguard stability by following proven guidelines:

- **Keep Expressions Modular** – Rather than cramming multiple nested statements into one line, break complex logic into smaller fields or named virtual columns for clarity and reuse.
- **Document Your Conditions** – Provide comments or maintain a reference sheet describing each workflow's purpose, trigger, and outcome to help team members navigate the logic.
- **Monitor Performance** – Observe load times, especially when multiple expressions evaluate simultaneously. Avoid unnecessary computations by referring to virtual columns only when needed.

CONCLUSION

Dynamic expressions and conditional workflows elevate your AppSheet apps from simple data repositories to fully automated solutions. By creatively harnessing logic and triggers, you can orchestrate complex processes with minimal user effort and deliver highly tailored experiences. In the next chapter, we'll further refine these capabilities with performance-driven approaches, exploring Slices and Security Filters to keep your app both fast and secure.

Chapter 4: Optimizing Performance with Slices and Security Filters

When dealing with large datasets and complex business logic, performance can become a critical factor in your AppSheet applications. Slices and Security Filters offer powerful ways to ensure that each user loads and interacts with only the data they need, minimizing unnecessary processing and speeding up your app's responsiveness. In this chapter, we'll explore strategies for effectively leveraging these features to achieve enhanced performance without compromising your application's functionality or security.

UNDERSTANDING THE ROLE OF SLICES

Slices act as specialized views of your underlying data tables. Instead of downloading and displaying every record to each user, you can create rules that extract only relevant subsets. This not only increases overall speed but also gives you granular control over how data is presented and managed for different roles or use cases.

- **Targeted Data for Different Views** – By applying conditions, you can isolate records needed for specific workflows. For example, a slice can show only "active projects" rather than all historical data, trimming load times significantly.
- **Differentiated User Interfaces** – Map slices to unique views for various user groups. A manager might see a broader range of information compared to a front-line team member who only needs a limited dataset.
- **Dynamic Slices** – Combine expressions with user attributes to tailor each slice based on the current user's identity (e.g., region, department). This approach ensures minimal overhead while still offering personalized data.

CRAFTING EFFICIENT SLICE CONDITIONS

To maximize performance gains, your slice conditions should be both precise and well-tuned. Complex expressions might slow down the query, so balancing your logic is key. Observe these tips when building slices:

- **Index-Focused Conditions** – If your data is stored in a SQL database, consider how your slice will interact with existing indexes. Columns that are frequently referenced in slice filters can be prime candidates for indexing.
- **Avoid Excessive Nesting** – When you layer multiple *OR* or *AND* statements, AppSheet processes each nested condition. Simplify where possible or break down logic into smaller, more manageable slices.
- **Test Efficiency with Temporary Slices** – Create test slices to confirm performance gains. Start with narrower conditions and broaden or refine them based on real-world usage and load times.

EMPLOYING SECURITY FILTERS FOR ROW-LEVEL SECURITY

Beyond performance, Security Filters ensure that each user only downloads and sees the rows they are allowed to view. This approach prevents sensitive data from ever reaching a device's cache, providing compliance benefits alongside speed enhancements.

- **Server-Side Filtration** – While slices hide data at the display level, Security Filters actually keep data from traveling to the user's device. This is especially crucial for sensitive or personally identifiable information.
- **Personalized Access** – Filter rows based on user attributes stored in your user table (e.g., department codes). Each user only sees relevant records, saving memory and bandwidth.
- **Dynamic Role Checks** – Utilize expressions that check the user's role or group membership in real-time, ensuring that security policies respond immediately to changes in user status.

BALANCING SLICES VS. SECURITY FILTERS

You can use Slices and Security Filters in tandem for a holistic solution. A critical decision is determining when to employ each feature:

- **Use Slices For UI Segmentation** – If you want the same table to power multiple views but display subsets of data depending on context, a slice is typically sufficient. Keep in mind, however, that all data still downloads to the device if there's no Security Filter.
- **Use Security Filters For Sensitive Data** – If you must ensure that certain records never reach unauthorized devices, you should limit the dataset with a Security Filter. This approach also enhances app speed by reducing data transfer.
- **Combine For Complex Requirements** – Often, you'll have both performance and confidentiality needs. Employ Security Filters at a high level to restrict overall data, and then refine user-facing views with layered slices.

CREATING COMPOSITE CONDITIONS

Complex organizations frequently require layered logic, such as role-based security combined with geographic constraints. By creating composite conditions in your Security Filters or slices, you ensure data remains smaller in scope and precisely matches each user's permissions:

1. **Role + Region Filtering** – Check if a user's role is authorized, then further narrow data based on their

assigned territory, ensuring each user can only access records from their designated region.

2. **Time-Based Access** – In certain workflows, older records may need to be archived or protected. Security Filters can keep historical data off standard user devices while still offering slices for occasional manager-level audits.

3. **Combined Constraints** – Nested expressions and references let you cross-check multiple columns and even external data sources. Keep expressions as efficient as possible to avoid performance penalties.

PERFORMANCE ANALYTICS AND MONITORING

As you layer on slices and filters, it's important to gauge their impact. AppSheet equips you with performance profiling tools to monitor synchronization times and identify possible bottlenecks:

- **Sync Duration Breakdowns** – Examine how much time the app spends downloading data versus processing logic. If the download portion is high, more aggressive filters may be needed.
- **Conditional Testing** – Experiment with different filter structures in test environments. Compare the sync times of simpler vs. more intricate conditions and adjust accordingly.
- **Server Resource Planning** – In enterprise settings, you might expand your database infrastructure. Collaborate with your IT team to ensure that your slicing logic aligns with indexing, partitioning, and other database optimization tactics.

LEVERAGING MULTI-LEVEL SECURITY PRACTICES

Beyond row-level security, consider additional layers to reinforce both data protection and performance:

Technique	Benefit
Column-Level Security	Hide sensitive fields (e.g., salaries, personal identifiers) from users who don't need them, further shrinking data transfer.
Secured App Formulas	Keep certain calculations in the back-end, so the app only loads precomputed results, reducing device-side workload.
Partitioned Tables	Physically separate data into smaller segments, applying distinct Security Filters to each partition for added focus and speed.

PRACTICAL TIPS FOR IMPLEMENTATION

Implementing Slices and Security Filters effectively requires iterative testing and a clear understanding of user needs. Here are a few practical suggestions:

- **Start with Broad Conditions** – Begin by separating large, obvious data categories (e.g., Active vs. Inactive) with slices or filters. Then refine as you gain clarity on usage patterns.

- **Reevaluate Regularly** – Business rules, staff roles, and data volume evolve. Schedule periodic checks of your filters to confirm they still match current operational needs.
- **Involve Stakeholders** – Consult top users or department heads to identify essential data for daily workflows. Fine-tune your approach to remove anything that's unnecessary or redundant.

CONCLUSION

Mastering slices and Security Filters is a critical milestone in advancing your AppSheet apps. By intelligently curating which records are downloaded, processed, and displayed, you maintain both speed and security as your datasets grow. As you proceed with building more complex solutions, these performance optimizations form the backbone of a responsive, scalable environment—where every user interacts with the data they genuinely need, without compromising system efficiency or confidentiality.

Chapter 5: Using Advanced Virtual Columns for Complex Calculations

Virtual columns hold a pivotal role in AppSheet applications, offering a means to dynamically calculate values without storing them physically in your dataset. While standard virtual columns might sum up totals or provide simple numeric fields, advanced techniques can unlock complex transformations, conditional outputs, and even predictive insights. This chapter explores how to fully leverage virtual columns for sophisticated calculations in order to create more powerful, data-driven AppSheet solutions.

ENHANCING CALCULATIONS WITH NESTED EXPRESSIONS

One effective way to expand the capabilities of virtual columns is to stack multiple expressions in a single formula. By nesting functions, you can produce precise results that incorporate diverse data points:

- **Layered IF Functions** – Control the flow of logic by checking successive conditions. For example, you can create a virtual column that calculates alternative tax rates depending on a product's category or location.
- **Combination Operators** – Blend arithmetic operations (like *+, -, */*) with logical operators (*AND, OR, NOT*) to orchestrate precisely the result you need.
- **Logical Shortcuts** – Employ *SWITCH()* or *IFS()* statements as streamlined alternatives to cumbersome nested *IF()* chains, improving clarity and readability.

REFERENCING DATA FROM MULTIPLE TABLES

AppSheet lets you pull values across tables to fuel your calculations—potentially drawing on data from parents, children, or even external sources. Advanced referencing can connect essential context to each row in real time:

- **Cross-Table Lookups** – Incorporate expressions that retrieve related record details, such as *[Related Orders][InvoiceAmount]*. This way, a single virtual column can reflect a comprehensive view of your app's data matrix.

- **Conditional Aggregation** – Combine *SUM()*, *AVG()*, or *COUNT()* with selective filters. For instance, sum the amounts of all child records in a certain status (e.g., "Open") to generate dynamically updated totals.
- **Multi-Path Connections** – Reference multiple relationships at once. Pull in data from one table to use as a calculation factor, then output results tied to another table, fostering a high degree of interactive logic.

IMPLEMENTING ADVANCED DATE AND TIME CALCULATIONS

Many businesses rely on date and time fields for scheduling, tracking service-level agreements, or logging events. Virtual columns can perform intricate computations on these fields, creating a more efficient flow of data:

- **Performing Interval Analysis** – Calculate time differences between two dates to gauge project lengths, response times, or compliance metrics. Use *HOUR()*, *DAY()*, or *WEEKDAY()* in synergy with *DATEDIF()* for robust tracking.
- **Rolling Date Windows** – Identify upcoming due dates or recently concluded schedules with dynamic logic. A virtual column can highlight tasks labeled "Within the Next 7 Days" or "Overdue by More Than 2 Weeks."
- **Forecasting and Projections** – Pair date calculations with numeric logic (like estimated hours per workday) to project completion dates or resource availability, elevating how your app supports planning activities.

AGGREGATING LARGE DATA SETS EFFICIENTLY

Handling bigger data collections calls for performance-conscious design, even when generating on-the-fly virtual fields. Strategic use of aggregation ensures quick results while preserving accuracy:

- **Selective Slices** – Pre-filter data through slices so that virtual columns operate only on relevant segments. This approach speeds up calculations and keeps focus on the most pertinent datasets.
- **Structured Summaries** – Use grouped or hierarchical representations. For example, sum monthly sales by region and then gather those results in a top-level virtual column for an executive overview.
- **Incremental Computations** – In fast-changing datasets, updating smaller pieces can be less demanding than recalculating everything each time. Break out partial computations into multiple virtual columns and integrate them step by step.

POWERFUL TRANSFORMERS USING APPSHEET FUNCTIONS

Beyond numeric or date transformations, advanced functions can reshape text, blend lists, and refine data to fit specific operational needs:

Function	Description	Use Case Example

SPLIT()	Splits a textual string into an itemized list based on a specified delimiter.	Handling CSV data in a virtual column and iterating through each item for processing.
TEXT()	Converts numeric or date-type data into formatted strings.	Creating clear date/time stamps for templated reports or email messages.
LIST()	Combines multiple values into a single list structure for further manipulations.	Assembling multiple child references or conditional results into a user-friendly summary field.

CHAINING VIRTUAL COLUMNS TO DRIVE MULTI-STEP OUTPUTS

Sometimes, you need sequential transformations to break down a complex calculation. This is where multiple virtual columns can build on each other for streamlined orchestration:

- **Stepwise Formulas** – Let one virtual column do initial parsing or partial sums, then feed its result into a second virtual column. This modular design keeps your calculations transparent and easier to manage.
- **Reusing Results** – Reference any virtual column just like a physical field. If a user modifies related data, AppSheet updates each dependent column automatically, ensuring live feedback.
- **Parallel Logic Paths** – You can develop different chains of virtual columns that each serve unique business rules. For instance, one chain might address

financial calculations, another might specify inventory restocking triggers.

DEBUGGING AND PERFORMANCE CONSIDERATIONS

While advanced virtual columns enhance functionality, they can also complicate troubleshooting if you're not mindful of performance. Keep these considerations at the forefront:

- **Incremental Testing** – Build complex expressions gradually. Confirm each portion in AppSheet's expression tester to identify potential syntax errors or logic bugs early on.
- **Keep It Modular** – Excessively long formulas with nested references can slow down sync times. Splitting massive calculations into smaller, reusable expressions often yields better maintainability.
- **Monitor Performance Logs** – Use AppSheet's performance tools to measure the time each virtual column requires to compute. If certain operations repeatedly strain the sync process, consider re-architecting or caching partial results.

CONCLUSION

Advanced virtual columns provide a robust way to handle intricate logic, dynamic aggregations, and multi-layered data transformations within AppSheet. Whether you're calculating specialized metrics, extracting values for custom dashboards, or orchestrating sequential workflows, leveraging virtual columns at a higher level can dramatically expand your application's capabilities. By thoughtfully designing modular expressions, referencing data across tables, and optimizing performance, you'll create virtual columns that power deeper insights and guide ever more sophisticated business processes.

Chapter 6: Leveraging Automation and Scheduled Bots

Automation stands as a powerful resource within AppSheet's advanced toolkit, enabling apps to perform tasks intelligently and consistently with minimal manual intervention. By supplementing on-demand processes with scheduled actions, you can eliminate redundant tasks, maintain data accuracy, and allow your team to focus on higher-value work. In this chapter, we'll delve deeper into harnessing AppSheet's Bots—especially those triggered on a set schedule—to craft polished, self-maintaining applications.

EXPANDING CAPABILITIES WITH MULTI-STEP BOTS

A single Bot can orchestrate multiple steps, each carrying out targeted actions in response to an event or scheduled trigger. Instead of creating one workflow per action, multi-step Bots consolidate logic in one place, providing a clear overview of the entire process. This structure not only keeps your app's logic organized but also simplifies debugging when parts of the workflow fail. Consider:

- **Sub-Processes for Data Updates** – Insert a step that sanitizes incoming data before moving to steps that create or modify related rows.
- **Branch-Driven Outcomes** – Use conditional branching within a Bot to direct the flow of tasks, such as notifying different teams depending on the data changes or sending varied communications based on priority.
- **Chained Actions** – Combine data updates, PDF generation, notification sending, and record archiving under one Bot for thorough coverage of a single event.

DESIGNING TIME-BASED AUTOMATION

Scheduled Bots allow you to kick off actions at specific intervals or times of day—an essential feature for tasks that don't hinge on user input. Whether you need routine data cleanup or timely reminders, time-based automation ensures consistency:

- **Daily Summaries** – Gather and email daily performance metrics each morning to keep leadership up-to-date without manual reporting.
- **Weekly Archiving** – Relocate or label older records at the end of each week, ensuring that active users only see current or relevant data.
- **Month-End Calculations** – Execute profit-and-loss computations or run inventory checks on the last day of each month to streamline financial or operational closures.

APPLYING EXPRESSION-DRIVEN FILTERS

Bots that run on scheduled triggers often benefit from filtering which rows—or sets of rows—are processed. By incorporating expressions, you precisely define which data falls under your Bot's domain:

- **Targeted Rows** – Use an expression that pinpoints only incomplete tasks, overdue invoices, or other subsets needing automatic intervention.
- **Dynamic Date Logic** – Couple time-based triggers with date fields to perform tasks on items that are reaching an expiration date or have remained idle for too long.
- **Role-Conscious Automations** – When a certain user group or department is responsible for an action, weave role checks into the filter so your Bot acts exclusively on the correct items.

REFINING NOTIFICATIONS AND COMMUNICATIONS

Scheduled Bots frequently handle large-scale notifications to keep stakeholders informed. Crafting clear, targeted messages expands user engagement and eliminates overload:

- **Conditional Recipients** – Set up logic so that only relevant teams or individuals receive notifications. For instance, only project managers get advanced performance alerts, while operations staff gets inventory updates.
- **Personalized Messaging** – Pull in keys or user attributes to customize subject lines and email content,

making the communication feel more direct and easier to act upon.
- **Multi-Channel Approach** – Depending on urgency, combine email, in-app notifications, and SMS messages under one Bot to maximize reach.

ERROR HANDLING AND FALLBACK SEQUENCES

Even robust scheduled Bots can encounter hiccups—such as database connectivity stalls or unexpected data anomalies. Advanced Bot designs include fallback steps to recover gracefully:

- **Retry Logic** – Set up an alternate action that re-attempts the original task after a specified delay if the first try fails.
- **Detailed Logging** – Maintain a separate record of Bot runs and any encountered issues, along with timestamps, so you can proactively address recurring errors.
- **Escalation Paths** – If an error persists, automate a message to a more senior team member, or trigger a different Bot that handles manual review before continuing.

PERFORMANCE CONSIDERATIONS FOR HIGH-VOLUME AUTOMATIONS

With complex scheduled tasks running across a large dataset, Bot performance can be critical. Advanced strategies can help you maintain smooth operations:

- **Slice-Based Processing** – Restrict Bot actions to focus on only the most relevant rows. This minimizes overhead and speeds up completion times.
- **Distributing Schedules** – Instead of a single massive Bot, break tasks into multiple scheduled Bots staggered throughout the day, avoiding simultaneous heavy loads.
- **Database Optimization** – Index frequently-used columns and regularly archive or partition data so that scheduled Bots operate efficiently, even under rapid growth conditions.

STRATEGIC BOT GOVERNANCE

When numerous Bots are active, particularly in enterprise environments, it's worth establishing clear governance practices:

- **Document Intent and Ownership** – Keep a reference describing each Bot's function, its schedule, and who is responsible for updates. This helps avoid overlapping automations or unintended data changes.
- **Lifecycle Management** – Periodically review whether Bots remain relevant. Retire or repurpose those that no longer serve a current business objective.
- **Access and Permissions** – Only grant Bot editing rights to authorized individuals. Mistakes or malicious updates to scheduling can disrupt critical processes or compromise data security.

CONCLUSION

By strategically leveraging automation and scheduled Bots, you reduce manual overhead and harness AppSheet's real-time data syncing to keep your organization aligned and informed around the clock. Thoughtful design—from filtered row targeting to error-recovery safeguards—turns repetitive procedures into efficient, consistent operations. As your application grows, these automations will evolve into the backbone of your workflow, ensuring daily tasks, routine checks, and crucial updates unfold reliably.

Chapter 7: Deep Dive into User Roles and Permissions

Assigning and managing user roles is critical for advanced AppSheet applications that handle sensitive information or require complex delegation of tasks. By carefully defining roles and responsibilities, you can offer each user a tailored experience, prevent unauthorized data access, and streamline app workflows. In this chapter, we'll explore the various methods AppSheet provides for configuring user access, how to align roles with security requirements, and best practices for maintaining clarity and control over permissions.

UNDERSTANDING THE ROLE CONCEPT

User roles establish bounds for what each individual can view, edit, or act upon within your application. These roles might range from "Standard Users," who are only allowed to modify their own records, to "Administrators," who manage the entire dataset and oversee global settings. By applying role-based security, you ensure:

- **Data Protection** – Limit the potential for accidental or intentional misuse by restricting access to information and actions only to those who legitimately need them.

- **Compliance Assurance** – In regulated industries, role-based permissions can help maintain audit trails and uphold data privacy obligations, like HIPAA or GDPR.
- **Streamlined UI** – Customize the visible menus, forms, and actions for each role, ensuring users encounter only relevant components and experience less clutter.

DEFINING ROLES AND PERMISSION LEVELS

To use AppSheet's role management effectively, you'll typically store user details in a dedicated table or leverage your organization's existing identity provider. From there, you can build out multiple permission levels, such as:

- **Read-Only** – Access to view data but not edit or create new records.
- **Contributor** – Can add and modify specific records, often limited to their departmental or personal scope.
- **Manager** – Oversee a broader subset of data, approve or reject workflow steps, and monitor team activity.
- **Admin/Owner** – Manage global app settings, user onboarding, and full data editing privileges.

Align these definitions with real-world responsibilities in your organization. A well-planned structure makes it easier to expand or revise roles later without disrupting everyday operations.

TAILORING CONTENT WITH CONDITIONAL LOGIC

Once you define roles at a high level, expressions and conditional settings fine-tune which forms, views, and actions each user can access. Consider:

- **Show_If Conditions** – Insert role-based logic (e.g., *[UserRole] = "Admin"*) in the Show_If property of key columns or views to hide them from non-admins.
- **Editable_If Rules** – Lock down sensitive fields by verifying the user role. A finance-approved role might edit billing fields, while a standard user is restricted to basic data entry.
- **Dynamic Actions** – Display specialized buttons, such as "Bulk Update" or "Reset Password," exclusively for roles that possess the authority to perform those tasks.

IMPLEMENTING ROW-LEVEL PERMISSIONS

Sometimes, it's not just about table-level or app-wide privileges. You might need different users to only see certain rows. This tight control is often vital in high-security or privacy-sensitive environments. Here's how to apply it:

- **Security Filters** – Combine role attributes with row-based conditions to ensure the dataset downloaded to a user's device contains only rows they should see (e.g., data tagged with their assigned region or department).
- **Ownership Fields** – Match each record to a user or group. By tying this back to the user's credentials, you funnel record visibility to only those entries the user owns or is explicitly allowed to manage.

- **Multiple-Access Criteria** – Use advanced expressions if multiple roles have partial access to the same data. For example, a manager might see all rows across their team, and a regional supervisor might see any row within their assigned region.

LEVERAGING CENTRALIZED USER TABLES

A dedicated table for user information can form the backbone of role-based security. Proper design lets you reference user details anywhere in your app:

- **Single Source of Truth** – Store username, role assignment, region, and other relevant attributes in one table for easy maintenance.
- **User Profile Enhancements** – Expand the table to include user preferences, contact info, or specialized attributes (e.g., certifications, skill levels) that may influence dynamic logic.
- **Cross-Reference in Expressions** – Seamlessly pull custom fields (like a user's project IDs) to filter data or shape how certain features appear to them.

PRACTICAL GOVERNANCE STRATEGIES

Complex role setups can become unwieldy over time, especially when new team members join or business needs shift. To keep your system manageable:

- **Role Naming Conventions** – Adopt consistent names (e.g., "Ops_Manager," "Sales_Associate") and avoid ambiguous labels that could create confusion during audits or expansions.

- **Granular Documentation** – Maintain a reference of which roles exist and their capabilities, so new admins or stakeholders can quickly identify who has access to what.
- **Review Schedules** – Periodically revisit roles and active users to remove obsolete accounts, merge redundant roles, or grant new restrictions based on emerging requirements.

AUTHENTICATING USERS AND INTEGRATING WITH SSO

For larger organizations or those with a robust IT infrastructure, single sign-on (SSO) integration simplifies user access and ensures enterprise-level security protocols are upheld:

- **Building SSO Bridges** – Connect AppSheet with identity providers like Azure AD or Google Workspace, automatically pulling role or group info from your directory.
- **Unified Onboarding** – New hires gain assigned roles in the central directory, instantly reflecting in AppSheet without the hassle of manual duplication.
- **Automatic Offboarding** – Once a user is removed from the organization's identity system, their app access ends simultaneously, minimizing the risk of orphaned accounts.

TESTING AND VALIDATING ROLE ASSIGNMENTS

Once your user roles and permissions are set, thorough testing helps prevent unexpected access gaps or errors:

- **Impersonation Scenarios** – Temporarily log in as different user roles to verify each role's permitted actions and data visibility in real time.
- **Edge Case Verification** – Check less common scenarios, such as a user with multiple overlapping roles or one lacking the role assignment entirely, to confirm your logic holds.
- **Review Security Logs** – If available, analyze any built-in app or identity provider logs to confirm no unauthorized access attempts slip through your configuration.

CONCLUSION

Advanced user role management stands at the heart of any data-sensitive and collaborative AppSheet environment. By mapping real-world responsibilities to role definitions, applying row-level filtering, integrating with enterprise identity systems, and thoroughly documenting and testing configurations, you gain the agility to adapt to new security requirements and organizational structures. As your apps evolve, these robust permissions practices will help you uphold consistent standards, maintain clarity for each user's function, and safeguard your datasets with confidence.

Chapter 8: Building Custom UI with Advanced UX Techniques

A visually appealing and user-friendly interface can greatly elevate how people engage with your AppSheet solutions. By leveraging the platform's advanced UX configurations, you can craft custom layouts, interactive controls, and visually guided navigation. In this chapter, we'll explore strategies for building unique experiences that cater to specific audiences and use cases, going beyond basic views to deliver a polished, high-performing app.

EMBRACING ADVANCED VIEW TYPES AND LAYOUTS

AppSheet offers multiple view templates—like Deck, Gallery, and even Map views—that you can tailor with refined options to emphasize your data in meaningful ways. By combining various view types with creative formatting, you'll pave smoother user paths and add depth to your app's visual design.

- **Dynamic Deck Views** – Show key details at a glance by controlling which fields appear and in what order. Incorporate progress bars, status icons, or color highlights to depict data states vividly.
- **Enhanced Gallery Displays** – Use high-resolution images as tiles for navigational or promotional elements, ensuring each tile showcases the most pertinent information, such as product details or user photos.

- **Contextual Map Overlays** – For location-based data, layered map views with custom pins can highlight service areas, event venues, or sales territories, allowing quick location-based interactions.

OPTIMIZING DASHBOARDS FOR MULTI-PANEL EXPERIENCES

Dashboards let you present different data sources or views in a single, consolidated screen. Beyond basic dashboards, advanced techniques can help you synchronize panels, enhance usability, and showcase critical metrics side by side:

- **Interactive Panel Linking** – Configure your dashboards so selecting a row in one panel draws related details or charts in adjacent panels. This synchronous layout enables real-time context without navigation overhead.
- **Adjustable Panel Sizes** – Experiment with adaptive layouts to give priority to crucial data segments. For instance, enlarge the panel showing a live chart of key performance indicators and reduce secondary panels to deliver a clear hierarchy of focus.
- **Role-Aware Panels** – Dynamically alter the panels available in a dashboard based on user permissions. Managers might see a budget summary panel, while individual contributors view personal task boards.

REFINING FORMS WITH CUSTOM INPUTS AND GUIDANCE

Forms remain a vital touchpoint for data capture and updates. Improving your forms with advanced UI elements and conditional logic can significantly reduce user error and boost satisfaction:

- **Multi-Step Inputs** – Split lengthy forms into multiple screens or use headings and sections to guide users progressively. This approach breaks complex data entry into bite-sized steps.
- **Inline Validation Prompts** – Implement quick feedback by showing error messages or status icons the moment an invalid entry occurs, preventing confusion or unexpected form rejections upon submission.
- **Conditional Sections** – Use *Show_If* expressions to hide or reveal fields based on the user's choices. For example, display shipping details only if an order requires physical delivery.

ELEVATING BRANDING THROUGH COLOR SCHEMES AND STYLING

A cohesive branding aura can make your app look more professional and reinforce organizational identity. Layering advanced design elements makes for a polished experience:

- **Custom Themes** – Select colors that align with your corporate palette. AppSheet's theme options allow you to manipulate header, text, and highlight accents, ensuring consistency across views.

- **Consistent Typography** – Use consistent font sizes or styles for titles, labels, and data fields to retain visual alignment and bolster readability.
- **Logos and Icons** – Include relevant logos in header areas or as icons in your menu. Swap standard icons with personalized ones to craft a distinct user environment.

IMPLEMENTING INTERACTIVE ACTIONS AND NAVIGATION

While standard menus and tabs can be sufficient, advanced apps often thrive with purpose-built actions and navigational flows that adapt to user input:

- **Action Buttons** – Embed action buttons in details views or forms for immediate next steps—like marking a record as approved or generating a quick PDF summary.
- **Deep Links** – Guide users directly to specific records, filtered dashboards, or external URLs from within your app. This technique streamlines complex journeys into one-click solutions.
- **Conditional Navigation** – Automatically route users based on role or data states. For instance, after saving a form, redirect managers to a dedicated approval page, while other users return to the main menu.

ENHANCING DATA VISIBILITY WITH FORMATTING RULES

Formatting rules allow you to color-code rows, highlight important text, or display icons based on app logic. By weaving these rules into your design strategy, you add intuitive cues to help users scan content efficiently:

- **Threshold Indicators** – Enlarge, bold, or color values that pass critical limits—such as inventory dropping below safety stock or tasks marked as "High Priority."
- **Iconography** – Use icons to convey status at a glance, like check marks for completed items or warning symbols for pending approvals. This visual shorthand can consolidate data into an easily identifiable icon library.
- **Gradients and Color Ladders** – Apply gradient color scales in numeric columns to reflect relative magnitudes, giving quick insight into ranges of performance or levels of completion.

COMBINING EXPRESSIONS FOR DYNAMIC UI ADJUSTMENTS

Just as expressions can drive data logic, they can also control how or when certain UI elements appear. With more advanced expressions, you automate user interactions:

- **Real-Time Visibility Checks** – Show or hide menu items based on user identity, device type, or the existence of specific child records. This granularity keeps your interface streamlined.
- **Usage-Based Triggers** – If certain fields meet specified values, switch your view or automatically direct the user to a follow-up page. This is especially handy for step-by-step workflows.
- **Adaptive Filters** – Craft vantage points that adapt to each user's last accessed data, role attributes, or even user-entered criteria, producing a customized, context-aware layout.

PRACTICAL TIPS FOR UI TESTING AND ITERATION

As you integrate advanced UX techniques, it's essential to test with target audiences to refine and optimize design. Consider these suggestions for continuous improvement:

- **Gather Early Feedback** – Let a small user group experiment with new UI elements before full rollout. Their input reveals friction points or thoughtful additions you may have missed.
- **Embrace Analytics** – Track user activity logs or measure how quickly tasks are completed in your newly enhanced forms or views. This data informs if your changes lead to tangible efficiency gains.
- **Explore Dark and Light Modes** – Offering dual themes can accommodate personal user preferences or mobile device settings, ensuring better accessibility in different lighting environments.

CONCLUSION

Elevating your app's user interface is far more than a cosmetic endeavor—it can streamline complex tasks and bring critical insights to the forefront. By applying specialized view types, dashboards, forms, color schemes, and navigation tactics, you transform interactions into an intuitive, engaging experience. As your app evolves, continuous feedback loops and iterative refinements will help keep your user interface fresh, functional, and aligned with business goals.

Chapter 9: Multi-Language Apps and Localization Strategies

Building applications that cater to a global audience or multilingual teams can significantly expand your AppSheet projects. Localization involves adapting not just the language displayed, but also formats, user input expectations, and cultural nuances. In this chapter, we'll explore strategies for designing multi-language apps in AppSheet, along with best practices to ensure your app remains intuitive and culturally relevant, regardless of the user's preferred language.

UNDERSTANDING THE IMPORTANCE OF LOCALIZATION

Localization extends beyond simple text translation; it considers factors such as currency symbols, date and time formats, and the direction of text (especially for right-to-left languages). By thoughtfully incorporating these elements, developers can create an inclusive experience for users worldwide, ensuring your application communicates effectively and respects local conventions.

- **Enhancing User Engagement** – Users are more likely to engage with apps in their native language and familiar regional formats.
- **Reducing Errors** – Presenting data in culturally appropriate ways (e.g., correct numeric separators or date layouts) limits confusion or misinterpretation.

- **Expanding Market Reach** – Localized apps open avenues for international clients and partners, enabling collaboration across multiple regions.

PREPARATION: DESIGNING A LOCALIZATION-FRIENDLY DATA MODEL

Before you begin translating or adding regional nuances, it's helpful to establish a flexible data structure. This often includes setting up tables or columns designed to hold translated text and environment details. Consider these approaches:

- **Localized Text Columns** – Instead of having a single *Label* or *Description* column, create multiple fields for each target language (e.g., *Description_EN, Description_ES, Description_FR*). This allows you to store parallel translations of the same piece of data.
- **Reference Tables** – For larger apps with numerous text strings, craft a dedicated table mapping a single key to multiple language versions. Reference these mappings in expressions to dynamically pull the correct translation.
- **Master Key Values** – Maintain a master key for each text snippet (e.g., a short code like *"WELCOME_MSG")* that anchors the translations, simplifying future modifications or addition of new languages.

IMPLEMENTING LANGUAGE SELECTION

One of the core challenges in multi-language apps is storing and referencing the user's preferred language. With AppSheet, you can integrate this choice into your user profile or data entries:

1. **User Profile Table** – Have a column indicating the user's chosen language (e.g., "English," "Spanish," "French"). Reference this column to conditionally display relevant translated fields throughout your app.
2. **Language Picker UI** – Provide a dropdown menu where users can manually select or change their language preference. Combine *Show_If* settings to ensure the rest of the app automatically reflects their new choice.
3. **Fallback Logic** – If a user's language setting doesn't match an actively supported language, default to a widely accessible option (e.g., English). This strategy preserves usability if your translations remain incomplete.

DYNAMICALLY DISPLAYING TRANSLATED FIELDS

Once you have translations in place, you'll need to instruct AppSheet which version of any given text to show based on user preferences. Expression-based techniques can streamline this process:

- **Conditional Display** – For forms or detail views, use an expression like *IF([UserLanguage] = "ES", [Description_ES], [Description_EN])*. This directs AppSheet to pick the correct field automatically.

- **Virtual Columns for Readability** – Create a virtual column that merges multiple translated columns into a single dynamic output. This helps manage references to text fields in other areas of your app.
- **Dedicated Slices** – In some cases, you can design separate slices for each language to filter specific content. This approach can be more relevant if the regions or user roles overlap with language groups.

ADDRESSING DATE, TIME, AND CURRENCY FORMATS

Localizing language is one piece of the puzzle; properly formatting numerical and date-type data according to regional conventions further enhances precision and clarity:

- **Regional Date & Time Formats** – If your users come from multiple regions, apply *TEXT()* expressions to shape date/time fields into the local standard (e.g., "DD/MM/YYYY" vs. "MM/DD/YYYY"). Consider the 24-hour clock vs. 12-hour clock for times.
- **Currency Localization** – When dealing with pricing or monetary amounts, incorporate local currency symbols and appropriate decimal separators. A single app might need to convert or display multiple currencies simultaneously.
- **Decimal Separators** – Some regions use the comma as a decimal separator. In advanced use cases, you might convert numeric outputs or inputs with expressions to mirror user preferences or system constraints.

SUPPORTING RIGHT-TO-LEFT LANGUAGES

Arabic, Hebrew, and other right-to-left (RTL) scripts require additional fine-tuning. While AppSheet supports basic display of these languages, you should explore strategic layout adaptations to optimize the user experience:

- **Evaluate Layouts Thoroughly** – UI elements, such as tables or forms, may need mirrored placement or reversed navigation flows. Conduct real-world tests with native speakers to confirm clarity.
- **Consistent Alignment** – Align text, icons, and labels so that they respect RTL reading patterns. If you rely heavily on images or icons, verify they don't conflict visually with text directions.
- **Conditional UX Rules** – Switch certain alignment or styling properties when *[UserLanguage]* is flagged as an RTL language, ensuring uniform design across all languages.

AUTOMATING TRANSLATION MAINTENANCE

As your app evolves, adding new features or refining existing texts is inevitable. Keeping translations in sync can be arduous without a plan:

1. **Centralized Translation Table** – Minimize reliance on scattered *Description* fields. Use a single source-of-truth table for every translatable string, referencing it throughout your app. A quick update here propagates changes everywhere.

2. **Bulk Uploads or Exports** – When you have translators or bilingual staff, creating a CSV or spreadsheet of your translation table can streamline the process, letting them update phrases en masse without sifting through your entire design.
3. **Integration Options** – For more complex scenarios, consider external translation APIs or version-controlled files. This approach can be particularly useful in large-scale or enterprise-level applications that undergo frequent localization updates.

TESTING AND VALIDATION

Quality assurance in a multi-language app goes beyond verifying that words appear translated. Rigorous testing ensures all text remains legible and that workflows are unaffected:

- **Role-by-Language Testing** – Combine role-based logic with localization checks. For instance, confirm that a manager in a Spanish-speaking region sees manager-level text in Spanish, including advanced form fields and dashboards.
- **Layout Stress Tests** – Certain translations might be longer or shorter than your source language. Validate that your UI adjusts gracefully to text expansion or contraction without cutting off content.
- **End-User Feedback** – Encourage bilingual or multilingual users to review critical paths in the app. Their familiarity can catch subtle nuances or culturally incorrect translations that automated or dictionary-based translations might miss.

PERFORMANCE CONSIDERATIONS IN LOCALIZATION

While storing multiple translations can enlarge datasets, careful strategies help maintain efficiency:

- **Security Filters** – If only certain user groups need specific languages, apply row-level filters so that unnecessary columns or translation rows don't load for every user—particularly useful when serving large user bases.
- **Conditional Computations** – Offload complex formatting or conversion to the database level when possible, thus minimizing repetitive calculations in virtual columns at the client side.
- **Incremental Rollouts** – Introduce additional languages gradually, monitoring sync times and user feedback to spot potential bottlenecks or areas requiring further optimization.

CONCLUSION

Enabling multi-language functionality alongside robust localization strategies can broaden your application's reach, foster a welcoming atmosphere for diverse user bases, and reduce error-prone data processes linked to cultural nuances. By planning your data model to incorporate multiple translated fields, implementing automated workflows for translation upkeep, and testing thoroughly for each language context, you lay a strong foundation for a truly global AppSheet experience. Whether your users require subtle region-specific date formats or total language overhauls, the techniques discussed here will help you craft a well-structured solution that comfortably bridges linguistic boundaries.

Chapter 10: Integrating External APIs for Expanded Functionality

Integrating external APIs can significantly expand the breadth of your AppSheet application's capabilities. By connecting to outside services, you can pull in data from specialized platforms, trigger events in third-party systems, or incorporate new functionalities that don't exist natively in AppSheet alone. In this chapter, we'll explore overarching design decisions, best practices, and advanced techniques to help you create robust, secure, and performance-driven API integrations within your apps.

WHY EXTERNAL APIS MATTER

AppSheet excels at organizing data within spreadsheets, databases, and cloud storage, yet many businesses rely on external web services for tasks like payment processing, social media engagement, or complex analytics. Integrating external APIs bridges your AppSheet environment with these specialized domains, effectively turning your application into a unified hub of information and workflows. With well-structured API calls, you can:

- **Automate Cross-System Tasks** – Push newly created records to finance apps, or retrieve up-to-date temperature readings from an IoT device.

- **Enhance Data Quality** – Pull validation rules or reference details directly from external experts (e.g., product catalogs, currency exchange tables).
- **Expand User Engagement** – Integrate chatbots, geolocation services, or messaging APIs to deliver a rounded, interactive experience.

ESTABLISHING THE RIGHT INTEGRATION MODEL

Before you start writing any calls, determine the simplest yet most effective way to connect. Each scenario will differ based on your external service's capabilities and your desired user experience. Common integration models include:

- **Webhook Calls** – Many APIs support inbound or outbound webhooks, triggering an URL that passes data in a JSON format. AppSheet's Workflow or Bot features can fire these webhooks based on user actions or scheduled events.
- **Custom Connectors with Scripts** – Employ Google Apps Script, for instance, to wrap complex API interactions in a structured way. Your AppSheet app then taps into that script for consolidated, reusable logic.
- **Third-Party Integration Tools** – Platforms like Zapier, Integromat, or Microsoft Power Automate can serve as intermediaries, bridging AppSheet events with APIs that don't have direct, user-friendly endpoints.

HANDLING AUTHENTICATION AND SECURITY

Security is paramount when exposing or accessing external resources. Depending on your use case, you might deal with credentials, API keys, OAuth tokens, or other sensitive information that must be handled carefully. Consider these practices:

- **Store Keys Securely** – Never hardcode API keys within public-facing expressions. Instead, use a secure data source or encrypted environment variables, if possible, to keep credentials out of plain sight.
- **Token Rotation** – Some APIs expire tokens after a set duration for security reasons. Build in logic to refresh or replace these tokens automatically, so your integration remains stable over time.
- **Use HTTPS** – Always encrypt data in transit by using HTTPS endpoints, especially if you're sending user or payment data through external services.

CRAFTING EFFECTIVE API REQUESTS

Designing your request payload and structure is a crucial part of external integration. A well-formed request ensures the service recognizes your data and can respond accurately:

- **Data Formats and Encoding** – Familiarize yourself with JSON, XML, or URL-encoded formats. JSON is particularly prevalent, so it's beneficial to understand how to assemble and parse it using expressions in AppSheet or external scripts.

- **Rate Limits** – Many APIs cap the frequency of requests. Identify these thresholds so you don't risk throttling or bans. When dealing with large volumes, consider batching calls or scheduling them at intervals.
- **Dynamic Fields** – In advanced use cases, you might pass user-selected data or table references. Ensure your request templates can flex if users change their inputs or if the structure of your app evolves.

ORCHESTRATING API CALLS WITH WORKFLOWS AND BOTS

AppSheet's workflows and automation Bots excel at triggering events in response to add, update, or delete operations. Here's how you can blend these tools with external API integrations:

- **Conditional Webhooks** – Create rules that send a webhook to an external service only when a record meets specific criteria (e.g., status changes to "Approved"). This precision eliminates redundant calls.
- **Multi-Step Bot Sequences** – Incorporate multiple actions in a single Bot scenario—e.g., send data to an external endpoint, wait for a response, then update another field in AppSheet to reflect the outcome.
- **Error Handling Steps** – Insert fallback pathways in case of an API failure. These may involve retrying the request, sending an alerts email, or reverting partial changes in your data.

RECEIVING AND PARSING EXTERNAL DATA

In addition to sending data to external systems, you may also need to fetch information and bring it back into AppSheet. Some scenarios include retrieving shipping quotes, currency rates, or inventory statuses:

- **Scheduled Imports** – Through Bots that run on timed intervals, you can periodically call external endpoints and store the responses in the appropriate tables. This is especially useful for daily or hourly updates from external databases.
- **Response Parsing** – For JSON payloads, tools like Google Apps Script or third-party connectors help transform the returned data into rows or columns that neatly fit your existing data model.
- **On-Demand Lookups** – If real-time data is needed, consider "Actions" tied to user clicks that trigger on-the-spot API calls. The results can populate new fields or display in a detail view.

VALIDATION AND ERROR MANAGEMENT

When moving data beyond AppSheet's native environment, you introduce more complexity and potential points of failure. Proper error handling ensures that data integrity and user confidence remain high:

- **Success/Failure Indicators** – Designate columns to reflect the status of API calls. For instance, store the message "Success" or "Error" along with relevant timestamps to keep track of every external transaction.
- **Retries and Queues** – In high-volume or mission-critical environments, set up a queue system where failed calls are retried automatically, possibly after a short delay or error resolution step.
- **User Alerts** – Alert the relevant users or admins when external integration issues arise. This might include a custom email, SMS, or an in-app notification with instructions or logs for troubleshooting.

PERFORMANCE OPTIMIZATION AND SCALABILITY

Each new integration can potentially slow down sync times or increase operational overhead. By optimizing your approach, you maintain an agile, scalable system:

- **Minimize Unnecessary Calls** – Restrict event-driven triggers to essential records and data changes. Overly frequent calls can consume bandwidth and risk hitting rate limits.
- **Caching Strategies** – Store evergreen or semi-static data sets locally for a set duration. This approach decreases repetitive lookups and speeds up user experiences, particularly with popular but rate-limited APIs.
- **Batched Requests** – For large data transfers, try grouping multiple updates in a single API call where supported. This consolidation can significantly reduce overhead and round-trip latency.

EXPERIMENTAL INTEGRATIONS AND FUTURE ENHANCEMENTS

The scope of external APIs continues to grow, offering everything from machine learning insights to advanced geospatial queries. Pushing the limits of integration might involve:

- **AI and ML APIs** – Incorporate natural language processing, predictive modeling, or image recognition services to automate decision-making or classification inside your app.
- **IoT Device Management** – Connect with smart devices or sensor networks, letting AppSheet users control parameters or glean real-time environmental data for advanced reporting.
- **Blockchain and Smart Contracts** – Though still emerging, some use cases may benefit from decentralized tracking or transaction validation anchored to blockchain APIs.

CONCLUSION

External API integrations offer a powerful means to merge disparate data sources and functionalities into a cohesive AppSheet ecosystem. By crafting secure, well-structured calls, orchestrating them through Bots, managing authentication responsibly, and diligently handling errors, you can elevate your application from a simple data manager to a truly interconnected platform. Whether you're pulling financial records from a payment gateway or pushing updates to a project management suite, these strategies ensure that your external API interactions flow reliably, securely, and in harmony with the rest of your advanced AppSheet configuration.

Chapter 11: Working with Webhooks for Automated Data Sharing

Webhooks can serve as a vital component in building advanced and interconnected AppSheet applications. They allow you to push data and events automatically to external systems, enabling real-time updates and streamlined collaboration between apps. By harnessing webhooks, you can reduce the need for manual exports or scheduled imports and instead let your app inform other platforms the moment changes happen. This chapter explores strategies for configuring, securing, and optimizing webhooks to achieve robust, automated data sharing in your AppSheet projects.

WHY WEBHOOKS MATTER IN MODERN WORKFLOWS

A webhook is essentially a user-defined callback URL that listens for specific events. When a relevant trigger occurs, an HTTP request is sent to this URL with details of the event or data changes. Unlike periodic synchronization methods, webhooks keep processes lean by acting immediately and only when needed. Here's what makes them invaluable:

- **Immediate Responses** – Eliminate time lags by communicating updates to external systems the moment they happen in AppSheet.
- **Bursting Past App Boundaries** – Let your apps share data with cloud services, internal endpoints, or even partner systems, paving the way for end-to-end workflow integration.
- **Lower Overhead** – Instead of hammering external APIs for the latest data, consume fewer resources by only sending relevant notifications when records change.

CONFIGURING WEBHOOKS IN APPSHEET

AppSheet provides direct webhook capabilities through its automation features, letting you construct workflows or Bots to push data outward upon specific triggers. Below are key considerations as you set up these connections:

- **Identify the Target Endpoint** – Obtain the exact URL from the service or system you're notifying. Often, these URLs come with parameters or keys pre-embedded to authenticate the request.
- **Select the Right Trigger** – Choose from add, update, or delete events, or combine multiple conditions if you need granular control (e.g., only sending a webhook when a field transitions from "Draft" to "Finalized").
- **Construct the Payload Structure** – Format and map out which columns or data fields will be included, typically in JSON format. A well-structured payload ensures the receiving system interprets your data accurately.

EVENT-DRIVEN ARCHITECTURES WITH WEBHOOKS

Introducing webhooks into your AppSheet apps can turn static processes into event-driven workflows. Instead of building a one-way integration, think of webhooks as a piece of a broader ecosystem:

- **Multi-Step Sequences** – After sending a webhook, an external service might process the payload and return a response or trigger a subsequent action. This chain reaction reduces manual intervention.

- **Parallel Notifications** – It's possible to broadcast a single data change to multiple webhook endpoints—updating internal systems, partner applications, and alert channels all at once.
- **Two-Way Flows** – A well-designed architecture can pair incoming webhooks from external apps (if they support them) with outbound webhooks from AppSheet, enabling real-time data interchange.

ENSURING SECURITY IN WEBHOOK DATA TRANSFERS

Data shared via webhooks must remain protected against unauthorized access and tampering, especially if it contains sensitive or regulated information. Consider these best practices for secure deployments:

- **HTTPS Encryption** – Always send webhook data over HTTPS to protect it while in transit. This is fundamental for maintaining confidentiality and integrity.
- **Secret Validation Tokens** – Some systems provide you with security tokens that you include in the header of your webhook request. The receiver checks this token to confirm authenticity.
- **Role-Based Triggers** – If certain data should only be visible to users with specific roles, wrap your AppSheet automation logic with restrictive conditions that limit the fields or rows sent out via the webhook.

OPTIMIZING PAYLOAD DESIGN

The content of your webhook request can make or break the usefulness of your integration. Too much unnecessary information can clog logs, while missing data forces secondary queries. Follow these guidelines for payload efficiency:

- **Focus on Change-Only Fields** – If you're tracking incremental changes, highlight only the updated columns instead of dumping the entire record every time a minor attribute changes.
- **Use Formats Familiar to the Receiver** – JSON is the most common format, but if the receiving service prefers form-encoded data, adapt accordingly to make parsing seamless.
- **Version Your Payloads** – If you anticipate future adjustments to the message structure, include a version number or schema reference so external systems can handle changes gracefully.

ENHANCING RELIABILITY WITH RETRY AND ACKNOWLEDGMENTS

Webhooks inherently rely on stable networks and responsive endpoints. Issues like server downtime can cause notifications to get lost or delayed. To mitigate these scenarios:

- **Enable Retries** – If a webhook fails or times out, configure limited retry attempts. This ensures that temporary server glitches don't interrupt critical data flows.
- **Expect Acknowledgments** – Some receivers reply with a success status code (2xx) when they properly process a request. Record this success code in your system to track the chain of custody for each data update.
- **Bolt-On Alerting** – If repeated retries fail, send an alert or log an error message. This allows administrators to investigate promptly before data discrepancies accumulate.

TESTING AND DEBUGGING WEBHOOKS

When implementing webhooks, issues can arise from incorrect payloads, endpoint mishandling, or incomplete triggers. Thorough testing is key to maintaining stable performance:

- **Use Mock Endpoints** – Services like *RequestBin* let you temporarily capture webhook requests, making it easier to validate that your payloads contain the correct data and formatting.
- **Check Logs and Headers** – Inspect any request headers, timestamps, and raw payload contents to debug alignment with the receiver's requirements.
- **Controlled Live Runs** – Gradually roll out actual webhooks in a development or sandbox environment, then escalate to production once reliability is confirmed.

EXPANDING CROSS-APP COORDINATION

Webhooks open the door to sophisticated multi-app ecosystems. You can merge data streams from different departments or external partners without creating tight coupling:

- **Automated Syncing with CRM or ERP Systems** – The moment a user updates customer data in AppSheet, your CRM receives the new information and keeps the entire organization aligned.
- **Notifications to Messaging Platforms** – Need to post real-time notices to collaborative hubs like Slack or Microsoft Teams? A webhook can automatically publish relevant updates in team channels.

- **Microservice Integrations** – If your company relies on microservices, each microservice can subscribe to relevant events from AppSheet, enabling a robust and scaled-out architecture.

FUTURE-PROOFING YOUR WEBHOOK STRATEGY

As your business evolves, so will the demands on your automation framework. Webhook strategies should be designed with flexibility in mind:

- **Declarative Configurations** – Whenever possible, store webhook URLs and parameters in configurable tables rather than hardcoding them. This allows quick updates or environment adjustments without major code changes.
- **Scalable Infrastructure** – Frame your receiving endpoints (if under your control) for high concurrency, so that spikes in AppSheet transactions don't overwhelm your service.
- **Event Prioritization** – Not every change demands an immediate webhook. Distinguish critical events from routine ones to prevent flooding external systems with low-value notifications.

CONCLUSION

By skillfully implementing webhooks, you can empower your AppSheet deployments to engage in near-instant conversations with outside platforms. From real-time status updates to seamlessly orchestrated workflows, webhooks play a pivotal role in turning otherwise isolated applications into dynamic, ever-connected solutions. With attention to payload design, security enhancements, and redundancy measures, your webhook-driven automations will function reliably and scale alongside your organization's growing data-sharing needs.

Chapter 12: Enhancing Scalability with Database Best Practices

As your AppSheet solutions mature, so do the demands on the databases that house your data. While small-scale apps can thrive on straightforward table structures, larger or rapidly growing projects benefit greatly from database strategies explicitly designed with scalability and performance in mind. By adopting best practices that address storage efficiency, query optimization, and transaction handling, you can future-proof your AppSheet implementations and ensure they continue to perform reliably under heavier loads and evolving business needs.

STRATEGIC PARTITIONING AND DATA DISTRIBUTION

Splitting large tables into distinct segments—by region, date range, or department—can help distribute data more effectively. This technique, known as partitioning, permits faster queries on subsets of data and can dramatically decrease load times for high-traffic apps.

- **Time-Based Segments** – Divide records by months or years so that legacy data can remain archived or read-only, freeing up resources for today's information.

- **Geographical Partitions** – In region-specific applications, isolate data based on location. Users in one area only interact with the appropriate dataset, minimizing excessive scans.
- **Flexible Allocation** – Adapt partition boundaries as your data profile changes. What begins as a monthly split might need weekly or daily partitions if growth rates spike.

INDEXING WITH PURPOSE

Indexes act like book chapter references, guiding query engines to the precise details they need. Creating the right indexes can save substantial time when your app retrieves data or applies filters.

- **Composite Indexes** – Combine multiple columns into one index to support typical queries. For example, if your users often filter by customer and date, a multi-column index can speed this task.
- **Selective Indexing** – Rather than indexing every column, focus on the ones most frequently used in filters or sorts. Over-indexing can slow writes and complicate maintenance.
- **Covering Indexes** – A well-designed index can "cover" the columns needed by a query and eliminate the need to look up the main table. This is especially beneficial for frequent read operations.

OPTIMIZING QUERIES WITH DATABASE VIEWS

For advanced applications, database views can help unify or simplify data with minimal overhead. Use views to pre-join or pre-aggregate data relevant to your AppSheet app, reducing on-the-fly computations.

- **Pre-Aggregation** – Summaries—like totals per month, or real-time statistics—can be calculated once in a view rather than repeatedly within AppSheet expressions.
- **Logical Separation** – Views hide the complexity of underlying tables and relationships, making it easier for your team to integrate new data sources without rewriting queries.
- **Security-Aware Views** – Restrict certain rows or columns in a view, ensuring only the minimal data reaches AppSheet. Coupled with AppSheet's own security measures, this creates tighter access control.

STAYING CONSISTENT WITH TRANSACTIONS

Data integrity becomes increasingly important as you scale. If multiple concurrent processes modify records simultaneously, you risk conflicts, partial writes, or lock contention. Thoughtful transaction handling helps mitigate these issues:

- **Atomic Operations** – Bundle related changes into a single, atomic transaction. All updates succeed or fail together, preventing inconsistent records.
- **Optimistic Locking** – In environments where conflicts are rare but possible, use optimistic concurrency controls. If an update collides, you can retry without blocking other processes.
- **Row-Level Granularity** – When your database supports fine-grained locks, your operations only lock rows involved in a transaction, boosting concurrency for large-scale apps.

CACHING FREQUENTLY ACCESSED DATA

Caching can lift pressure from your core database by offloading repeated queries. While AppSheet itself implements synchronization logic, certain high-demand data might benefit from an alternative caching approach in your database layer:

- **Materialized Views** – A database can store a physically present snapshot of a query's results. When reading data, your system fetches from this snapshot rather than performing a resource-heavy calculation.
- **In-Memory Data Stores** – Tools like Redis or Memcached can hold key-value pairs in server memory. Queries that rely on frequently accessed references will respond quicker than going straight to disk storage.
- **Expiration Policies** – Periodically refresh caches to keep them accurate. Striking the right balance between read speed and data staleness is essential for sustaining reliability.

MAINTAINING CLEAR DATA RETENTION POLICIES

Accumulating excessive historical data can degrade performance over time. A well-outlined retention policy ensures your primary tables stay lean and relevant for day-to-day operations:

- **Archival Strategies** – Move older or closed records to a separate database or an archival table. Users or auditors can still search this data, but it won't slow down current transactions.

- **Tiered Storage** – Keep the most critical data on faster storage solutions, while lower-tier or historical information resides on cost-effective, slower mediums.
- **Compliance-Driven Purges** – Some industries mandate removing or anonymizing data after a set period. Align your database cleanups with these legal obligations and adjust your policy accordingly.

SCALING OUT: HORIZONTAL VS. VERTICAL APPROACHES

Preparation for high growth means understanding how you'll scale your database infrastructure. Two common approaches include adding more powerful servers (vertical scaling) or distributing data among multiple servers (horizontal scaling):

- **Vertical Scaling** – Increasing CPU, RAM, or disk capacity on a single machine can push immediate gains. However, there's a practical ceiling where improvements plateau or become cost-inefficient.
- **Horizontal Scaling** – Splitting the load among multiple database servers (e.g., through replication, sharding) can accommodate massive data volumes and user concurrency. This approach requires more complex coordination but often yields better long-term flexibility.
- **Hybrid Models** – Many organizations combine both strategies: scaling up to a certain point, then distributing data across shards or read replicas when single-server approaches approach their limit.

MONITORING AND TUNING IN REAL TIME

Even a well-planned database architecture benefits from continuous monitoring to catch performance bottlenecks early. Setting up analytics and logging tools lays the groundwork for proactive improvements:

- **Resource Dashboards** – Track CPU usage, memory consumption, and storage metrics. Sudden spikes might reveal inefficient queries or a data partition that's grown beyond expectations.
- **Query Profiling** – Enable slow query logs or use query analyzers to see which operations run most frequently or take the longest. Updating indexes or rewriting problematic queries can often yield immediate speed boosts.
- **Alerting Rules** – Configure automatic notifications whenever thresholds—such as read/write latencies—surpass acceptable limits. Quick intervention can prevent small issues from becoming show-stoppers.

HIGH AVAILABILITY AND REDUNDANCY

Organizations that depend on mission-critical AppSheet apps can't afford extended downtime. Investing in a robust redundancy plan ensures your app remains accessible, even if certain components fail:

- **Database Replication** – Keep live copies of your database on separate servers or data centers. If the primary server fails, a replica can quickly take over with minimal data loss.

- **Failover Mechanisms** – Implement automatic failover solutions that detect outages and reroute traffic to a healthy node, reducing manual intervention and downtime.
- **Load Balancers** – Distribute read requests among replicas, preventing any single node from becoming a bottleneck. Users experience seamless performance regardless of busy periods.

CONCLUSION

Establishing robust database practices is a cornerstone of scaling your AppSheet deployments. By employing targeted indexing, thoughtful partitioning, and strategic storage architectures, you ensure that data operations remain swift and dependable. When combined with reliable failover solutions, real-time monitoring, and purposeful data retention plans, you set the stage for an AppSheet ecosystem that can adapt to growing workloads and ever-evolving business requirements. With these database best practices in place, your advanced applications will continue to serve large user bases, deliver real-time insights, and operate efficiently even as they expand well beyond their initial scope.

Chapter 13: Creating Responsive Dashboards and Charts

Building effective dashboards and visualizations is vital for delivering quick insights into your AppSheet data. While tables and forms serve their purpose, charts provide an immediate, at-a-glance understanding of trends, relationships, or anomalies. In this chapter, we'll explore advanced techniques for designing dashboards that not only look appealing, but also dynamically respond to user actions and data updates—enabling faster decision-making and more interactive app experiences.

LEVERAGING ADAPTIVE DASHBOARD LAYOUTS

AppSheet's dashboard feature allows multiple views to coexist on the same screen. However, simply tossing grids and charts together might result in clutter. A well-structured dashboard places critical metrics in focus while allowing deeper exploration elsewhere. Key suggestions include:

- **Responsive Panels** – Configure panels to automatically resize or shift based on screen dimensions. This ensures your dashboard remains user-friendly whether on a mobile device, tablet, or large desktop monitor.
- **Prioritizing Layout Flow** – Place the most essential chart or key performance indicator (KPI) at the top or left side. Downstream panels can reveal supporting data or detailed breakdowns, creating a logical reading path.
- **Swappable Sections** – Use Show_If expressions to display certain sections only when relevant to a selected record or data filter. This dynamic approach helps declutter the screen for users who need laser-focused views.

SYNCHRONIZING DASHBOARD ELEMENTS

Interactive dashboards shine when each widget or chart automatically updates in response to user input—such as clicking on a record or applying a filter. Implement these techniques to maintain a cohesive and immersive experience:

- **Linked Views** – Configure a table or deck view to act as a "master," and connect it to charts or detail views as "children." Selecting an item in the master panel filters sibling panels accordingly.
- **Drill-Down Pathways** – Provide direct links on your charts so that when users tap a data point, the app navigates to a more detailed view or another dashboard showing granular context (e.g., a breakdown by product category).
- **Synchronized Slices** – Rely on expressions in slices that use the same filter criteria or user-defined input, ensuring all dashboard components share the same subset of data at any given time.

ADVANCED CHART CUSTOMIZATION

While AppSheet offers standard chart types (bar, line, pie, etc.), there are more nuanced ways to present insights and drive user engagement. Explore these customization techniques for a more polished result:

- **Layered Chart Definitions** – Combine multiple data series on the same chart to compare metrics side by side (e.g., target vs. actual sales). This visual overlay helps highlight discrepancies or alignments within a single graph.
- **Conditional Formatting** – Use data rules to emphasize key thresholds (e.g., color bars red if they exceed a danger level). Users can quickly spot outliers or items requiring urgent attention.
- **Customized Labels** – Leverage expressions to present user-friendly axis and legend labels. Instead of "Column001," ensure each label conveys meaningful terminology, elevating clarity.

REAL-TIME AND LIVE-UPDATING DASHBOARDS

In dynamic environments, dashboards that constantly refresh provide an immediate pulse on operational data. If your scenario calls for near-instant updates—like monitoring ongoing processes—consider these strategies:

1. **Frequent Sync Intervals** – By default, AppSheet syncs periodically or upon data edits. You can shorten intervals or encourage manual syncs if real-time awareness is critical, though be mindful of performance trade-offs.
2. **Automated Triggers** – Use AppSheet Bots to push data changes or refresh certain slices when conditions are met. This ensures charts always capture up-to-the-minute information.
3. **Optimized Data Sources** – Consider employing database views or materialized views for high-volume dashboards. Pre-aggregated data draws faster, mitigating lag while still delivering current metrics.

INCORPORATING USER-DEFINED FILTERS AND CONTROLS

Static dashboards can lose their utility if users lack the power to filter or pivot data independently. By granting interactive controls, your charts and tables become more potent for analytical deep dives:

- **Filter Fields** – Provide dynamic dropdowns or quick-select buttons referencing columns linked to your chart.

Users can swap categories, date ranges, or statuses, prompting immediate chart recalculations.

- **Searchable Inputs** – For text-heavy or ID-based data, embed a search box that allows users to find relevant records within the dashboard context, updating any connected charts or lists instantly.
- **User Role-Based Adjustments** – Enforce different filter scopes based on the logged-in user's role. Managers might see company-wide data, while contributors see only their project's details, all within the same dashboard framework.

MAKING USE OF MULTIPLE CHART TYPES

Not all data suits a single type of visualization. A combination of chart styles can reveal relationships and patterns that are otherwise hidden:

- **Bar or Column Charts** – Highlight comparisons or rankings among discrete categories (e.g., sales by region). Simple color coding or stacked bars can convey extended layers of information.
- **Line and Area Charts** – Depict trends over time, effectively illustrating seasonality, growth rates, or cyclical patterns. Overlay a goal line to emphasize variance from targets.
- **Pie and Donut Charts** – Ideal for a high-level breakdown of proportions, though keep them reserved for small sets of categories. Too many slices dilute clarity.

BALANCING PERFORMANCE WITH VISUAL COMPLEXITY

Complex dashboards can become sluggish if not tuned properly. While you want to impress users with data depth, speed and responsiveness should remain top priorities:

- **Efficient Data Sources** – Limit your charts to only the columns and rows truly needed. Slices or security filters ensure that each chart loads minimal data, reducing overhead.
- **Limit Overlapping Charts** – Display multiple charts only if each adds unique insights. Overlapping or redundant visualizations can bloat sync times and tax the user's device.
- **Progressive Loading** – If your dataset is massive, consider distributing visualizations across multiple dashboard tabs or sub-dashboards, so users reveal data only when relevant.

BUILDING STORYTELLING DASHBOARDS

A truly impactful dashboard doesn't just serve raw numbers—it guides the user through a narrative, highlighting key insights and prompting action. Effective storytelling might include:

- **Contextual Text Boxes** – Add short paragraphs or annotated metrics to guide interpretation. Labels like "This month's top-selling product" direct attention to crucial data points.
- **Trend Highlighting** – Use simple icons or color-coded arrows to denote positive vs. negative shifts, so users immediately sense urgency or success.

- **Action Buttons** – Let viewers respond to the insight. Whether it's approving a pricing change, drilling to a deeper analysis, or assigning tasks, bridging data to real actions ensures your dashboards fuel meaningful outcomes.

TESTING AND TROUBLESHOOTING DASHBOARDS

The successful rollout of a new chart or dashboard requires careful validation. Testing ensures performance remains stable and data accuracy is unwavering:

- **Device Variation Checks** – Ensure your layout remains engaging on smartphones, tablets, and desktops. Field test with real devices instead of relying solely on emulators.
- **Role-Specific Accounts** – Log in as different user roles to confirm each group sees the right scope and doesn't experience unexpected filters or missing panels.
- **Load Testing** – For dashboards that hundreds or thousands of users may access simultaneously, conduct load tests to measure sync times and identify potential data bottlenecks.

CONCLUSION

Responsive dashboards and charts contribute immensely to an app's end-user engagement and operational utility. By emphasizing adaptive layouts, synchronization between panels, and diverse visualization styles, you create data experiences that capture key insights at a glance. Whether you aim to offer real-time monitoring or an analytical deep dive, mindful design choices and attention to performance details ensure that your dashboards remain both compelling and efficient. In turn, these powerful visuals help stakeholders make informed decisions swiftly, keeping your AppSheet solution at the center of effective business operations.

Chapter 14: Advanced Actions and Nested Workflows

In multi-layered applications, coordinating actions and workflows can significantly increase efficiency and maintain consistency. Whether updating multiple records in a single step or orchestrating intricate sequences of approvals, advanced actions and nested workflows empower your app to mirror sophisticated real-world processes. Below are strategies for designing, managing, and optimizing these powerful capabilities.

ORCHESTRATING MULTI-STAGE PROCESSES WITH ACTION SEQUENCES

To deliver smooth workflows, many organizations rely on chaining separate tasks into one unified sequence. Instead of expecting users to perform several manual clicks or form entries, a single click can trigger multiple operations aligned to the logical flow of your process.

- **Concise Batch Updates** – By bundling dependent actions into one event, you ensure data consistency; for instance, when an item moves from "Open" to "Closed," you can automatically log completion and reset related child tasks.

- **Linking Across Data Tables** – If different units share responsibilities, your action sequences can target multiple tables. For example, updating a "Tasks" table might instantly propagate a revised status to a "Projects" table and a "Finance" table simultaneously.
- **Condition-Based Executions** – Enhance clarity by adding *IF* conditions within your action sequences. A single user command triggers only the relevant updates, preventing unintended changes or partial overwrites.

DESIGNING NESTED APPROVAL CHAINS

Complex business processes often require multi-tier approval. Rather than manually notifying each reviewer, nested workflows automate the transition from one approval to the next. This approach keeps all participants aligned, while ensuring each step remains transparent.

- **Tiered Roles and Responsibilities** – Route requests for initial review to supervisors, then move them up to directors as needed. Each completed step automatically triggers the subsequent reviewer's stage, so no request stalls.
- **Escalation Management** – In situations like delayed approvals, you can set timer-based actions that escalate the request if it remains pending beyond a threshold, ensuring items do not slip through the cracks.
- **Contextual Notifications** – Configure messages containing details of the specific stage. Recipients gain clear insights on what was approved previously, reducing back-and-forth clarification messages.

MANAGING WORKFLOW BRANCHES FOR DIVERGENT OUTCOMES

Some processes involve alternative pathways depending on user input, data values, or automated checks. Nested workflows with branching allow your system to handle varied scenarios with minimal manual direction.

- **Branch-Friendly Expressions** – Adopt *IFS*, *IF*, or *SWITCH* expressions to steer outcomes. If a condition is met, the workflow follows one path; otherwise, it routes to an alternative.
- **Parallel Actions** – In some models, multiple branches can run concurrently. For instance, finalizing a sales deal might roll out welcome emails to customers while separately notifying fulfillment teams.
- **Automated Cleanup** – Once a branch completes, your workflows can remove or update data no longer relevant. This preserves clarity for ongoing tasks, avoiding clutter in your application's dashboards and tables.

CHAINING WORKFLOWS VIA BOTS

Bots can serve as a framework for tying multiple workflows together, inserting decision points along the route. By consolidating everything under a single Bot, it becomes easier to track progress and maintain consistent logic.

- **Multi-Step Conditions** – A single Bot can check multiple conditions in sequence, choosing which workflow to activate at each juncture and reducing the risk of repetitive or conflicting triggers.

- **Linked Outcome Paths** – When one workflow finishes, its results can inform the next step. This ensures your entire process remains cohesive, eliminating gaps from data flagged at the previous stage.
- **Reusable Components** – If a nested workflow sub-process proves beneficial, incorporate it into different Bots or sections within your app without rebuilding from scratch.

SECURING AND MONITORING COMPLEX PROCESSES

As advanced logic grows, security must keep pace. By integrating authorization checks, logs, and error alerts, you prevent inadvertent data exposures or incomplete updates.

- **Role-Level Restrictions** – Enforce that certain advanced actions are only callable by specific user groups. This prevents unauthorized manipulations of critical data structures.
- **Error Visibility** – Log outcomes for each step, including failures. Alert designated administrators or process owners if a workflow halts unpredictably, so they can intervene quickly.
- **Track Evolving Dependencies** – While nested workflows might depend on external APIs or cross-table references, proactively handling connectivity or permission issues keeps your process predictable.

OPTIMIZING PERFORMANCE IN EXTENDED ACTIONS

Long-running, multi-step workflows can affect overall responsiveness. Efficiency becomes even more vital as stakeholder demands or data volumes expand.

- **Break Up Non-Critical Steps** – If an action is not time-sensitive, schedule it after high-priority tasks finish. Spacing out events avoids overloading your system and preserves a snappy user experience.
- **Cache Repetitive Lookups** – Reusing information from a virtual column or an indexed slice keeps quick calculations consistent, rather than recalculating the same dataset multiple times.
- **Monitor Sync Durations** – Track whether nested actions or compound workflows add incremental sync time. If so, refine step logic or consider partial updates at each stage.

STRATEGIC TESTING AND LIFECYCLE MANAGEMENT

Complex action chains benefit from rigorous testing protocols to ensure they reliably handle real-world scenarios. A structured lifecycle—covering development, testing, and deployment—keeps newly introduced logic stable.

- **Incremental Unit Testing** – First validate each individual action before stitching them into a larger workflow. Confirm that small parts work smoothly in isolated conditions to save future troubleshooting effort.
- **Sandbox Deployments** – Test nested workflows in a separate environment populated with representative

data. If any step misfires under heavy load, refine it before allowing broader access.

- **Evolution Over Time** – Build a plan for maintaining or updating advanced actions. As organizational processes shift or data structures evolve, revise your workflows consistently to reflect the latest requirements.

CONCLUSION

Advanced actions and nested workflows enable powerful, automated processes spanning multiple tables, users, and external touchpoints. By orchestrating chained steps, branching paths, and tiered approvals, teams can accelerate collaboration, reduce errors, and stay aligned with complex operations. Well-defined testing, user permission strategies, and ongoing performance checks help ensure these sequences remain both reliable and responsive. This synergistic combination of actions and workflows transforms your AppSheet application into a dynamic engine that adapts and scales as your business needs intensify.

Chapter 15: Handling Large-Scale Data Imports and Exports

Managing extensive data transfers is a pivotal aspect for many AppSheet implementations. As applications grow, you may need to incorporate large datasets from external sources or push bulk updates to other systems. Sizable imports and exports can pose challenges related to performance, data consistency, and user experience if not planned carefully. This chapter outlines strategies and practices for seamless large-scale data operations within AppSheet, focusing on reliability and scalability.

PREPARING FOR BULK IMPORT OPERATIONS

Successful large-scale data imports begin with thorough planning. Prioritize the integrity and structure of the incoming data, ensuring your AppSheet schemas are ready to handle the influx:

- **Schema Alignment** – Confirm that the incoming file or source data matches the table definitions in your app. Mismatched column headers or data types can cause partial failures or malformed records.
- **Incremental Importing** – When processing exceedingly large files, consider splitting them into smaller chunks. This diminishes risks associated with timeouts and can speed up processing on both the source and the AppSheet side.
- **Data Validation Steps** – Set up expressions or staging tables to validate data before merging it into your production tables. Catching errors early prevents faulty information from propagating throughout your system.

AUTOMATING BATCH IMPORTS

Manual imports can be cumbersome, especially if they occur frequently or involve thousands of rows. AppSheet's automation capabilities enable you to handle these tasks in a more systematic way:

- **Scheduled Bots** – Trigger imports at off-peak hours to reduce competition with daily user activity. By automating these workflows, you ensure consistent data refresh cycles, even if files arrive daily or weekly.

- **Pre-Processing Scripts** – If you utilize an intermediate tool or script to pull data from external APIs, you can cleanse and structure it prior to placing it in AppSheet-compatible formats, minimizing the chance of runtime errors.
- **Retry Mechanisms** – For imports susceptible to intermittent network or system errors, build a retry loop that resumes any interrupted segments. This approach provides reliability for critical or time-sensitive data.

MANAGING CONCURRENCY AND LOCKING

When multiple users or processes attempt to modify large amounts of data simultaneously, concurrency conflicts can arise. In high-volume use cases, consider additional safeguards:

- **Optimistic Concurrency** – Alert users if data has changed since they began an update, allowing them to reconcile differences before finalizing the import.
- **Queue-Based Sequencing** – Rather than allowing parallel imports, queue them in a logical order. Once one batch completes, the next begins, maintaining data stability and preventing partial overwrites.
- **Locking Sensitive Tables** – For mission-critical data, adopt short-term table or row locks during heavy imports. Though it can momentarily inhibit edits, it preserves data integrity for high-stakes workflows.

ENSURING DATA QUALITY DURING IMPORTS

Quality assurance steps are often overlooked when juggling massive data sets. Proactive validation helps maintain high standards in your AppSheet app:

- **Reference Lookups** – Cross-verify foreign keys against your existing tables to ensure that each imported record correctly maps to parent entities.
- **Conditional Checks** – Implement *Valid_If* conditions that reject or flag records with out-of-range values (e.g., negative quantities or invalid dates). Post-import scripts or Bots can move flagged items to a review table.
- **Comprehensive Audit Trails** – Log details about who performed the import, when it occurred, and how many records were added or updated. This traceability forms a crucial safety net for large-scale operations.

BEST PRACTICES FOR LARGE-SCALE EXPORTS

Exports come into play when you need to archive data, share it with clients, or feed another system. Handling large volumes requires attention to format, performance, and security:

- **Segmented Exports** – Export data in batches, using date filters or record limits for each segment. This reduces file size limits and upload or download times, particularly when dealing with tens of thousands of rows.
- **Secure Delivery** – If exporting sensitive information (financial records, personal data), encrypt files or transfer them through secure channels. You can

configure AppSheet to post data to a secure endpoint or cloud storage path.

- **Scheduled Archival** – Automate exports to run at structured times—end of day, weekly, or monthly— especially if other systems rely on your data. Coordinating exports ensures external partners or teams access timely information without manual intervention.

OPTIMIZING PERFORMANCE AND SYNC TIMES

Large imports and exports can strain your app's sync processes. Fine-tune your approach to mitigate slowdowns for everyday users:

- **Temporary Slices** – Isolate the scope of a big export by creating specialized slices, preventing extraneous columns or filters from slowing the operation. This approach also guards smaller tables from unnecessary overhead.
- **Off-Peak Scheduling** – Whenever possible, schedule large imports or exports outside peak usage. Minimizing competition for resources preserves responsiveness for other users still interacting with the app.
- **Background Processes** – If you integrate external scripts or APIs, run them in the background to avoid tying up the main app's interface. Bot notifications can inform stakeholders once the task completes.

RECOVERY AND ERROR HANDLING

Even well-designed processes can encounter snags—corrupted files, interrupted connections, or unexpected format discrepancies. Plan contingencies to handle these situations gracefully:

- **Rollback Mechanisms** – If errors surface midway, revert partially imported data to its pre-import state. This keeps your tables consistent and prevents users from interacting with incomplete records.
- **Error Logging** – Maintain a record of all warnings or failures encountered during the import or export. Provide actionable messages so administrators can quickly correct issues and rerun the process.
- **Commit in Stages** – Commit data in workable increments and verify each stage's success before proceeding. This strategy simplifies problem isolation if any subset of records causes errors or triggers duplicates.

CONCLUSION

By applying thoughtful techniques—ranging from chunked file handling to automated scheduling—AppSheet developers can comfortably manage large-scale data transfers without disrupting regular app operations. Rigorous validation ensures new data aligns with existing structures, while controlled export processes keep downstream systems and stakeholders informed. With careful execution and robust error recovery, these operations maintain high data quality, scale reliably alongside your growing user base, and preserve an efficient, robust AppSheet experience.

Chapter 16: Implementing Complex Security Models

Security is often a top priority for advanced AppSheet implementations that handle sensitive or proprietary data. While many applications require simple user-level or role-based restrictions, some business scenarios demand deeper granularity—like protecting columns containing confidential information, implementing tiered review processes, or enforcing stringent rules on specific device types. In this chapter, we'll examine how to craft complex security setups that go beyond basic role checks and embrace multi-layered defenses to keep your data safe.

DESIGNING MULTI-TIER SECURITY STRUCTURES

A multi-tier approach involves layering various security controls so that each level independently protects its portion of the system. This design minimizes the risk of a single failure triggering broader compromise.

- **Access Segmentation** – Segment user groups into refined tiers (e.g., "Analyst," "Supervisor," "Audit," "Executive") aligned with the real-world divisions of data ownership and authority.
- **Layered Checks** – Combine role-based security with row-level filters. Even if a user belongs to the "Manager" role, apply row restrictions that depend on additional attributes like department or region.
- **Independent Validations** – Use parallel rules for viewing, editing, and deleting data. A user might see a record but still require higher-level authorization to modify certain fields.

EMPLOYING ADVANCED COLUMN PROTECTIONS

In many scenarios, not all columns are created equal. Columns holding personal identifiable information (PII) or sensitive metrics must be carefully hidden or encrypted, even from certain authorized users.

- **Dynamic Show_If and Editable_If** – Beyond a simple "Don't show this column to everyone," add logic that checks user roles or conditions. For instance, only reveal employee salary columns to HR members with approved clearance.
- **Conditional Encryption** – If your data source supports encryption or you have an external service handling encryption at rest, enforce that columns with confidential data are encrypted. In AppSheet, combine with Show_If to limit who sees decrypted data.
- **Audit-Aware Columns** – Tag highly sensitive columns for audit trails. Whenever a user views or updates these fields, log the event in a secure location, providing an extra layer of accountability.

RESTRICTING DATA BASED ON DEVICE OR NETWORK

Advanced security models may mandate different levels of trust depending on where and how users access the application. If corporate policy forbids external access to certain data, AppSheet supports controls that adapt to device or connection context:

- **IP Address Constraints** – Pairing with your VPN or corporate network can limit full application functionality to known IP ranges. Once outside those ranges, only non-sensitive portions might remain accessible.

- **Device-Type Rules** – If mobile usage is riskier than desktop sessions, assign "read-only" to mobile roles, or permit editing solely on company-managed devices. This approach balances productivity with security concerns.
- **Time-of-Day Restrictions** – Some industries restrict data entry outside business hours for compliance or risk mitigation. By adding time-based checks, you ensure users can't inadvertently process data when oversight is limited.

IMPLEMENTING CONTEXTUAL DATA VISIBILITY

Beyond standard row filters, security can depend on dynamic context, such as the stage of a workflow or the content of specific columns:

- **Stage-Gated Visibility** – If your app has a multi-step process, you could hide certain elements until the user's stage is reached. For instance, a final approval screen remains hidden from mid-level staff until all prior tasks are complete.
- **Self-Learning Rules** – Over time, your application might record recurring conditions. You could automatically tighten security if data shows repeated attempts to access restricted columns, flagging suspicious patterns with triggers.
- **On-Demand Revelation** – Let managers or administrators provisionally grant access to specific records rather than entire tables. With a toggle, they can "unlock" a row for a short timeframe, then automatically revert to locked status.

CONSOLIDATING MULTIPLE AUTHENTICATION METHODS

For enterprise-scale deployments or third-party partner apps, you may combine Single Sign-On (SSO), OAuth, or internal directories, ensuring that each user's identity is uniformly recognized:

- **Federated Identity** – Link AppSheet authentication to a central identity provider (like Azure AD or Okta) that manages credentials and multi-factor authentication. This consistency keeps user role assignments synchronized across multiple applications.
- **Token-Based Access** – Instead of storing raw credentials, issue secure tokens that expire after a set period. AppSheet can check if the token is still valid before granting data access.
- **Fallback Credentials** – Provide alternative sign-in routes for remote contractors or temporary staff who can't join your main identity system. A limited-scope role ensures they never see restricted data.

AUTOMATING SECURITY FILTER UPDATES

As users shift departments or business rules evolve, your security filters must keep pace. Automations can relieve administrators from constantly updating complex conditions:

- **Event-Driven Modifications** – When a user's role changes, a Bot updates the relevant filters or row ownership in your user reference table. The new permissions reflect immediately, minimizing risk from delayed manual changes.

- **Scheduled Policy Checks** – Periodic Bots can scan user records. If someone is inactive for too long or a contract has expired, automatically reduce or revoke their privileges.
- **Self-Service Requests** – For large organizations, establishing a controlled form where managers apply for changes in user access ensures a transparent, trackable method of requesting and approving adjustments.

MONITORING AND LOGGING FOR FORENSIC ANALYSIS

Heightened security demands also imply robust logging. When sensitive data is involved, audits and forensic reviews help retrace digital footprints in case of anomalous events:

- **Session Logs** – Record user logins, data views, and IP addresses. If unusual access patterns appear, an alert can be triggered, allowing security teams to respond quickly.
- **Fine-Grained Access Logs** – For columns flagged "top-secret," log each user who expands or edits them. This detailed ledger reveals potential oversight gaps or suspicious access attempts.
- **Data Tamper Warnings** – Create a Bot that periodically checks record integrity. If unauthorized changes occur, the system can revert them or mark the data as "Compromised" until it's inspected.

BALANCING SECURITY AND USABILITY

Complex models sometimes frustrate legitimate users if they find themselves locked out of essential tools. Striking a balance between robust defense and efficient workflow is paramount:

- **Role-Focused Onboarding** – Provide an introduction for new hires or role transfers, detailing what they can and cannot access. With clarity comes fewer friction points and lower support overhead.
- **Contextual Error Messages** – If users attempt a restricted action, show them a concise explanation rather than a generic denial. Point them to a relevant manager or request form for further assistance.
- **Regular Security Audits** – Periodically gather feedback from end-users and security specialists. Fine-tune the model where excessive locking disrupts productivity or where potential loopholes exist.

CONCLUSION

Implementing complex security models in AppSheet entails mixing role-level permissions, granular column protections, dynamic data filters, and diligent monitoring to defend sensitive data. Whether you're controlling who sees a handful of critical fields or fortifying entire datasets with advanced authentication, a careful blend of layered defenses will elevate the resilience of your application. When paired with ongoing audits, automation, and user-focused clarity, your security model can safeguard even the most valuable or confidential information without impeding legitimate business operations.

Chapter 17: Debugging and Error Handling in AppSheet

As applications grow more sophisticated, so too do the possible points of failure. In AppSheet, mistakes can manifest in the form of misaligned expressions, workflow misfires, or data inconsistencies. Recognizing and swiftly resolving these glitches is crucial to sustaining a smooth user experience and minimizing downtime. In this chapter, we'll explore advanced strategies for diagnosing issues within your app and structuring your logic to gracefully handle potential errors.

IDENTIFYING ROOT CAUSES WITH SYSTEM LOGS

A fundamental step in debugging is pinpointing where a problem originates. AppSheet's built-in monitoring and log views are exceptionally helpful for uncovering the hidden layers of your app's operations. By carefully reading these logs, you can trace each user event, expression evaluation, and workflow execution.

- **Detailed Sync Logs** – Access logs that detail data sync operations. Check for synchronization failures or unexpected delays, which might point to issues in data filters, broken references, or conflicting updates.
- **Automation Audit Trails** – For complex Bots or workflows, each action is logged with triggers, conditions, and success or failure messages. Reviewing these logs helps isolate the exact step, condition, or data mismatch causing a misfire.

- **Timestamp Analysis** – Sorting log events by time can reveal the sequence of operations, clarifying if an unexpected expression error cascaded into additional breaks in subsequent actions.

REFINING EXPRESSIONS USING THE EXPRESSION ASSISTANT

Expressions often form the logic backbone of high-level AppSheet features—whether it's calculating totals, filtering records, or shaping dynamic rules. Even advanced developers occasionally battle misconfigured expressions. Fortunately, the Expression Assistant provides robust debugging help:

- **Step-by-Step Evaluations** – Break multi-layer expressions into smaller components. By testing fragments, you'll see intermediate outputs and more easily spot where an operator or condition fails.
- **Sample Value Testing** – Input different row values in the Expression Assistant's test area to see how your formula behaves across contexts (e.g., user roles, different statuses). This ensures edge cases are detected early.
- **Syntax Highlighting and Suggestions** – The Expression Assistant flags syntax problems and proposes relevant functions or fields. While small, these hints can prevent overlooked typos and type mismatches that spark downstream errors.

BUILDING FALLBACK SCENARIOS FOR ERROR HANDLING

While certain mistakes require developer intervention, smaller hiccups can be navigated automatically. By weaving fallback logic into your expressions, Bots, or workflows, you construct safety nets for common pitfalls:

- **Default Values** – When an expression fails or returns a null, define a sensible default to keep the rest of the process afloat. For instance, if a currency conversion API call fails, revert to a prior known rate rather than halting the entire workflow.
- **Conditional Skips** – In multi-action sequences, skip steps that aren't critical if they encounter run-time irregularities. Use expression checks (e.g., *IF(ISERROR([CalculatedField]), …)* to gracefully bypass trouble spots.
- **Graceful Notifications** – Alert relevant team members when a fallback route activates. This ensures they're aware of the temporary measure and can decide if deeper troubleshooting is necessary.

TESTING CHANGES IN A CONTROLLED ENVIRONMENT

Sudden changes in data structure or logic can inadvertently break existing features. Creating a safe, controlled environment for testing helps catch regressions before they reach end users:

- **App Copy for Experiments** – Clone your app and test new expressions or workflows in the copy. Once

111

validated, mirror the adjustments in production to avoid surprising disruptions.

- **Sample Data Sets** – Upload a small, representative set of data that covers edge cases and typical scenarios. This ensures you don't risk damaging live data during debugging, but still see how changes behave in realistic conditions.
- **Feature Flags** – In advanced setups, use user attributes or custom columns (e.g., "Beta Tester?") to selectively turn on or hide new features. This incremental rollout reveals snags early, among smaller user groups.

HANDLING CONCURRENT UPDATES AND CONFLICTS

Conflict errors surface when multiple users or processes simultaneously attempt to alter the same data. While AppSheet manages many concurrency details behind the scenes, advanced debugging can help minimize collisions:

- **Version Number Columns** – Storing a version or timestamp column in frequently edited tables helps detect if the underlying record changed between read and write operations.
- **Incremental Sync Strategies** – Encourage more frequent syncs or run background sync processes to keep user devices updated. This reduces stale data edits that lead to conflict errors.
- **Conflict Resolution Scripts** – Employ Apps Script or external processes to detect overlapping edits. If a collision is found, define a resolution rule (e.g., "latest edit wins" or "merge fields") to preserve critical data seamlessly.

PROACTIVE PERFORMANCE PROFILING

Major performance bottlenecks often masquerade as functional errors—long sync times can cause timeouts, leading to partial data updates or incomplete workflows. By proactive profiling, you prevent these hidden pitfalls from crippling your app:

- **Monitoring Execution Times** – Check performance statistics on AppSheet's performance panel. Track where the heaviest operations occur (e.g., slices, references, expressions) and refine them for efficiency.
- **Splitting Heavy Steps** – If a single workflow executes numerous data operations, break it into smaller sequences or time-triggered Bots. This approach lowers the chance of any single step stalling.
- **Relocating Complex Computations** – For extremely calculation-heavy tasks, consider precomputing them at the database level or via external scripts. AppSheet can then reference these results directly, speeding up user-facing interactions.

IMPLEMENTING TAILORED ERROR MESSAGING

Default error prompts can confuse users, leading to unnecessary support tickets or incomplete submissions. When you design custom error messages, you guide users through self-resolution:

- **Context-Aware Prompts** – If a user attempts to save without filling a mandatory field, specify *which* field is missing. This directness prevents them from hunting through multiple inputs.

- **Probable Solutions** – For more advanced issues—like an erroneous date range—suggest typical solutions: "Try ensuring the start date is before the end date." A clear next step reduces confusion.
- **Tiered Messaging** – If a problem might affect many users, embed a contact path ("Contact IT if you consistently see this error"). Let frontline staff handle smaller issues to minimize top-level disruptions.

ALERTING AND ESCALATION FOR CRITICAL FAILURES

Simple user-facing messages might not be enough for severe breakdowns—like core data synchronization halts or widespread formula corruption. In these scenarios, an automated escalation plan ensures swift intervention:

- **Bot-Triggered Notifications** – Program a Bot to watch for error keywords in logs or track the frequency of repeated failures. If thresholds are exceeded, the Bot emails or texts key team members for immediate action.
- **Fail-Safe Routines** – In the event of a complete workflow crash, revert critical columns or rows to their last stable state. This approach keeps the app partially operational until the root fix is deployed.
- **Centralized Incident Reports** – Maintain a dedicated table for high-severity incidents. Each record includes timestamps, relevant log snippets, and user context. This historical log fosters pattern detection to prevent future recurrences.

MAINTAINING A DEBRIEF AND CONTINUOUS LEARNING CYCLE

Each error or glitch becomes an opportunity to fortify your application. By capturing lessons learned and methodically refining your approach, you reduce the likelihood of repeated missteps:

- **Post-Mortem Reviews** – For major issues, hold a brief review to discuss root causes, timelines, and final resolutions. Document best practices discovered and integrate them into your development standards.
- **Shared Knowledge Base** – Encourage collaboration by listing common error patterns and their resolutions in a central repository. New team members can learn from prior experience instead of repeating old mistakes.
- **Preview Upcoming Changes** – Stay informed about new AppSheet features, especially those touching automation or security. Experiment with them in a safe environment to preempt breaking changes and incorporate updated debugging tools.

CONCLUSION

Debugging and error handling in AppSheet requires a synergistic mix of systematic testing approaches, in-depth log analysis, and thoughtfully structured fallback logic. By creating controlled testing environments, implementing thorough performance oversight, and designing intuitive yet potent error messages, teams can swiftly pinpoint the source of trouble—and keep their solutions running optimally. In an advanced development setting, these robust techniques ensure your application not only remains functional, but also becomes more resilient against future challenges.

Chapter 18: Deep Links, Navigation, and Custom Menus

Making an application easy to navigate is more than just good design—it's a strategic advantage. With AppSheet's deep links and custom menus, you can guide users to the exact screens or subsets of information they need, speeding up workflows and reducing confusion. This chapter explores how to leverage these navigation options to craft tightly focused entry points, contextual transitions, and tailored menus that cater to specific user roles or tasks.

UNDERSTANDING THE POWER OF DEEP LINKS

A "deep link" is essentially a direct URL-like reference that takes a user straight to a particular view, row, or filtered set of data in your AppSheet environment. Instead of making someone click through multiple screens, you offer a shortcut to the exact place they need to be. These links can be placed in notifications, emails, or other in-app elements to create a frictionless user experience.

Use cases for deep links span quick record lookups, one-click approvals, or even context-specific product pages. When combined with role-based logic or security filters, these links ensure that users only see permitted data, while still enjoying a seamless jump into the application's core features.

CONSTRUCTING COMPLEX NAVIGATION PATHS

In a data-driven app, standard tabs and views may not capture the evolving needs of every workflow. Complex navigation paths let you tailor journeys that adapt to variables like a user's role, region, or the current app status. For instance, one sequence may lead managers from a dashboard of high-level metrics directly into each region's performance analytics, while field employees might follow a different route highlighting operational tasks and quick logs.

Implementing these paths often involves expressions that check user attributes or form inputs, then decide where each action sends the user. By focusing on directness and relevance, you help individuals reach necessary information in fewer steps, preserving valuable time in busy environments.

BALANCING FLEXIBILITY AND SECURITY

Though deep links and sophisticated navigation bolster usability, they must align with your security model. A direct link should not bypass permission controls. For sensitive data, confirm that row-level and column-level security remain active, even if someone clicks a link from an email or chat message. This defense ensures that only authorized users can open protected views, mitigating potential data exposure.

Combining security filters, user roles, and link-based navigation gives you confidence that even if a URL is shared among colleagues, non-permitted users see no more than general or placeholder screens. This dual approach maximizes utility without compromising on data governance.

CRAFTING ROLE-SPECIFIC CUSTOM MENUS

Custom menus add a polished, intuitive layer to your user interface. Instead of relying on default navigation bars, you can create responsive "home" or "side" menus, each loaded with relevant options for a user group. For example, team leads might get menu items related to shift scheduling, escalations, and analytics, while field agents see action buttons for quick form entries and local tasks.

In constructing these menus, expressions come in handy for showing or hiding items based on the user's attributes. A carefully planned menu can reduce screen clutter and confusion, guiding each role toward the tasks they must handle most frequently.

ENHANCING MENUS WITH CONDITIONAL FORMATTING AND ICONS

Eye-catching icons and conditional formatting can further transform menus from static lists into vibrant signposts that direct attention where needed. Color-coding key sections or applying distinct icons for forms, reports, and dashboards quickly signals their function. Meanwhile, conditional logic can highlight menu items that require urgent attention (e.g., "Pending Approvals" in red if any requests are overdue).

By relying on icons and subtle color shifts, you encourage intuitive navigation. Users can rapidly find and interpret the options they want, fostering a smoother experience for newcomers and power users alike.

EMBEDDING DEEP LINKS IN WORKFLOWS AND EMAILS

Integrating direct links within automated communications greatly enhances workflow efficiency. Consider a scenario where an approval request email includes a button or hyperlink that takes the manager straight to the relevant record in AppSheet. One click, and the manager sees all the details needed to make a decision.

Likewise, in periodic summary notifications, you might embed links to specialized "review" screens that filter records by date or status. Recipients can jump right in, ensuring critical tasks step forward in real time, rather than waiting for the next login or manual search.

TESTING AND REFINING YOUR NAVIGATION FRAMEWORK

Deep links and menus can evolve quickly, especially as new features or user groups come online. Regular testing ensures that these elements remain seamless and well-organized. Periodically log in with different roles to verify the correctness of each destination. If a menu item leads to a stale or removed view, update the link or remove it for clarity's sake.

Gather user feedback on menu flow and direct links. If certain shortcuts see minimal usage, consider removing them or merging them into larger categories. The best designs focus on high-impact paths that reflect genuine business needs—leading to a fluid experience for all involved.

CONCLUSION

Deep links and custom menus elevate AppSheet applications beyond simple table-based navigation, granting precise control over user journeys. By carefully weaving direct links into workflows and providing menus tailored to each role, you enable streamlined access to critical tasks and insights. Even as your app grows more complex, dynamic expressions and conditional formatting keep navigation friendly and relevant. Whether you're connecting email recipients to fast approvals or driving specialized user groups to curated dashboards, these navigation features ensure your application remains both powerful and user-centric.

Chapter 19: App Lifecycle Strategies: Development, Testing, and Deployment

A successful AppSheet solution rarely remains static. As new features emerge and business requirements evolve, you'll revisit your app's design, trial changes, and eventually publish fresh versions to users in a controlled manner. Mastering the application lifecycle—from initial development to rigorous testing and seamless deployment—ensures that each new iteration balances innovation with reliability. By following well-defined processes, you minimize disruption, maintain data integrity, and deliver continuous value.

PLAN FIRST, BUILD LATER

A structured planning phase lays the groundwork for a smooth lifecycle. Rather than diving straight into development, consider sketching out new requirements, identifying potential data impacts, and clarifying which user groups might be affected:

- **Requirements Gathering** – Collect goals and features from stakeholders, focusing on practical enhancements. Pinpoint any areas that need compliance oversights or advanced security measures.
- **Task Prioritization** – Not every idea must land in the immediate release. Categorize requests by importance, feasibility, and urgency to shape a manageable roadmap.
- **Resource Allocation** – For larger organizations, designate who will handle each aspect of the build. Whether it's data structure updates or user interface tweaks, assigning ownership prevents gaps or duplication.

SANDBOXING FOR EXPERIMENTAL BUILDS

Experimenting with new features in a "production" environment can lead to accidental downtime or data inconsistencies. Instead, maintain a sandbox or development copy of your app to validate ideas before pushing them live:

- **App Copy Approach** – Duplicate your existing production app, ensuring it references either mock data or a separate test database. This way, changes won't affect real users.
- **Version Tagging** – Clearly label the cloned app so testers and collaborators know it's for experimentation. Distinct naming reduces confusion between stable and test versions.
- **Frequent Sync Checks** – Regularly review how modifications look and act within the sandbox. Early detection of UI or process anomalies simplifies refinements.

ITERATIVE TESTING ROUTINES

Even small tweaks benefit from thorough testing. By integrating iterative checkpoints, you catch errors early and keep development cycles efficient:

- **Unit Testing** – Validate each new feature in isolation. For instance, if you introduce a new form, confirm that required fields, default values, and conditional visibility behave as expected.
- **Role-Based Simulation** – Check how different users interact with changes. Operations managers and on-the-ground staff might uncover distinct glitches due to their custom views and security filters.
- **Boundary Tests** – deliberately push the limits of data ranges or user inputs. Overly large file uploads, unconventional date formats, or extreme numeric values may reveal hidden vulnerabilities.

PEER REVIEWS AND COLLABORATIVE FEEDBACK

Inviting fresh perspectives can unearth issues that solo developers miss. Peer reviews foster collective ownership and help ensure your updates align with broader organizational goals:

- **Design Walkthroughs** – Showcase interface changes or behind-the-scenes logic to colleagues, discussing how new tables, columns, or expressions integrate into the existing flow.
- **Chat and Comment Tools** – Encourage testers to annotate errors or confusion in real time. AppSheet's collaboration features—or external platforms like Slack or Microsoft Teams—can log suggestions quickly.
- **Cross-Functional Insight** – Business analysts might evaluate feature viability from a process standpoint, while IT or data teams can confirm security and scalability align with your roadmap.

STAGING AND CONTROLLED RELEASES

Once you're confident in your changes, it's time to transition from isolated experiments to a controlled pilot. A staging environment, or an "early access" version, lets a small group of users experience the new release under real conditions:

- **Limited-User Pilots** – Grant a select subset of experienced users or team leads access to the staging app. Gather their feedback on usability, performance, and stability before full rollout.
- **Gradual Feature Flags** – In advanced setups, toggling specific features on or off for certain roles allows quick

rollback if issues arise, limiting the blast radius of any unexpected behaviors.

- **Monitoring and Metrics** – Track synchronization times, error logs, and user satisfaction. If a spike in support requests emerges during staging, analyze trends to isolate root causes.

DEPLOYMENT AND POST-RELEASE MONITORING

The final step—deployment—exposes your fresh updates to every user. However, the process doesn't end once you flip the switch. Ongoing observation and fine-tuning ensure the app settles into a stable state:

- **Communicate Changes** – Inform users about new capabilities or interface modifications. Well-documented notes and brief tutorials reduce confusion and spotlight potential workflow efficiencies.
- **Real-Time Feedback Channels** – Equip users with a quick way to report anomalies (e.g., a dedicated "Report Issue" form or in-app chat). Prompt responses maintain confidence in the updated system.
- **Performance Checks** – Examine whether new features strain data sync volumes or slow critical workflows. If so, refine or schedule further optimization to preserve smooth performance.

CONCLUSION

Adopting a mature lifecycle approach fortifies your AppSheet projects against the pitfalls of haste or incomplete testing. Each stage—planning, sandboxing, thorough validation, and careful deployment—creates a safety net, ensuring that your innovations don't undermine stability. With clear communication and a willingness to gather feedback, you pave the way for smooth transitions and sustained user trust. As a result, your app evolves fluidly, consistently meeting new demands while upholding the polished reliability that stakeholders expect.

Chapter 20: Optimizing Collaboration in Cross-Team Environments

Collaboration within and across different teams is a critical element of building successful AppSheet applications at scale. When roles and responsibilities span various departments—each with its own workflows, resources, and priorities—you need strategies that harmonize efforts and streamline communication. By effectively synchronizing data, processes, and user engagement, you can cultivate an environment where teams collaborate seamlessly, reducing duplicate work and accelerating innovation.

ESTABLISHING CLEAR ROLES AND RESPONSIBILITIES

One of the first steps toward effective cross-team collaboration is to outline each participant's role within the project. Clarity around who manages data models, user experience, automation, and security helps minimize overlap and confusion.

- **Defined Ownership** – Assign a "Data Lead" to oversee database connections and table structures. Allow a "UX Specialist" to manage visual design, while one or more "Automation Coordinators" tackle workflows and bots.

These owners not only keep tasks organized but also ensure timely updates.

- **Role-Centric Training** – Provide targeted guidance for each role. A team focused on security might dive deeper into access controls and row-level filters, while those handling user interface can explore advanced formatting rules.
- **Handoff Protocols** – Develop a procedure for handing off changes from one role to another. For instance, if the UX team modifies a form layout, they alert the workflow creators in case new notifications or triggers are necessary.

VERSION CONTROL AND CHANGE TRACKING

Keeping track of changes in a multi-team environment is crucial. Without a plan for version control and documentation, minor updates can cause major disruptions if not communicated properly.

- **Incremental App Copies** – Before pushing critical changes, create a copy of your app. This serves as a "working branch," preventing unintended edits from impacting production. Once tested, merge those modifications into the main version.
- **Changelog Documentation** – After every significant update—be it a new table, workflow rule, or user interface tweak—log a brief summary of the change. This record helps teams quickly spot conflicts or revert if issues arise.
- **Scheduled Review Sessions** – Host regular (e.g., weekly or bi-weekly) meetings where teams present their recent changes. During these reviews, highlight any dependencies or feature overlaps that might affect other departments.

COORDINATING APP ARCHITECTURE WITH SHARED COMPONENTS

Multiple teams may require similar functionalities in their respective areas. Harnessing shared resources—like templates, expressions, and preconfigured workflows—can streamline collaboration.

- **Common Data Models** – Encourage departments to rely on shared reference tables (e.g., "Users," "Projects," "Clients") rather than duplicating them. This approach reduces data drift and promotes a single source of truth.
- **Reusable Expressions** – Collect frequently used expressions—such as conditional calculations or user role checks—into a centralized repository. Teams can reuse these snippets, ensuring consistency and speeding up development.
- **Unified Design Patterns** – Standardizing on certain design elements (color schemes, icons, or form layouts) across the app helps keep the user experience cohesive, even as different groups contribute custom features.

IMPLEMENTING STRUCTURED TEST CYCLES

Cross-team environments carry a higher risk of misunderstandings or oversights. Rigorous testing not only validates functionality within each department but also ensures overall compatibility.

- **Department-Specific Testing** – Each group tests its designated features thoroughly before any joint testing occurs. This step catches local issues early, preventing them from surfacing during larger integration checks.
- **Integration Sprints** – Organize periodic sync-ups where all teams perform combined tests. These "integration sprints" confirm that new features from one department don't inadvertently break workflows in another.
- **Feedback Loop** – Document user feedback from each test cycle. Update relevant features promptly, and communicate any constraints (e.g., security limitations) that might affect another team's development goals.

PROMOTING CROSS-TOOL VISIBILITY

Large organizations often use multiple systems—CRMs, project management tools, and communication platforms. Ensuring teams stay aligned means connecting these complementary systems into a transparent ecosystem.

- **Real-Time Dashboards** – Provide dashboards that blend data from multiple teams. A combined view showcasing project statuses, pending approvals, and upcoming deadlines reduces guesswork and fosters shared ownership.
- **Embedded Channels** – Integrate messaging apps (e.g., Slack or Microsoft Teams) with your AppSheet notifications. This setup allows cross-functional groups to receive timely updates in their common workflow channels.
- **External API Bridges** – When specialized tools host key data, configure secure API connections. By syncing records both ways (AppSheet ↔ external system), no group operates in a silo.

ENCOURAGING CONTINUOUS COMMUNICATION

Technical competencies alone can't guarantee success; collaboration flourishes when teams freely share knowledge. Establish open channels and a culture of active dialogue.

- **Regular Stand-Ups** – Short, frequent updates keep everyone informed of progress and roadblocks. If a department anticipates a new feature that could impact another's tasks, mention it early to adjust schedules smoothly.
- **Cross-Training Sessions** – Hold informal workshops where each department explains its segment of the app. Such knowledge exchange not only demystifies complexities but also highlights synergy opportunities.
- **Shared Documentation Platforms** – Host how-to guides, expression libraries, and design patterns in a central documentation repository. Encouraging updates from all departments maintains comprehensive, current references.

BALANCING AUTONOMY WITH OVERSIGHT

While autonomy gives teams the freedom to innovate, too much independence can splinter the overall solution. A moderate level of oversight keeps everyone on track without stifling creativity.

- **Architectural Review Board** – Form a group of senior members who periodically review major data schema changes, integration plans, and security decisions. Their role is to align upgrades with the bigger organizational roadmap.

- **Guided Autonomy** – Provide templates or style guides that teams can modify within defined limits. This approach ensures a consistent user experience while granting each group flexibility to tailor features.
- **Milestone Checkpoints** – Request review at predefined milestones (e.g., end of each sprint). This practice offers enough space for teams to be creative without risking misalignments that are difficult to fix afterward.

CONCLUSION

By nurturing well-defined roles, promoting transparent communication, and unifying development efforts, organizations can harness the collective strengths of various teams within an AppSheet project. Through disciplined version control, consistent testing, and a strong emphasis on shared resources, each department contributes to a robust and cohesive application suite. Ultimately, optimizing collaboration not only drives efficiency but also propels more innovative and impactful solutions—ensuring your AppSheet environment grows in harmony with the broader goals of the enterprise.

Chapter 21: Best Practices for App Performance and Speed

Performance is a critical success factor for any AppSheet deployment, especially as data volumes and user interactions grow. A slow or unresponsive app can reduce adoption and undermine business outcomes. Fortunately, there are strategic measures you can take to optimize speed and responsiveness. Below are best practices and techniques for refining throughput, minimizing latency, and ensuring your application remains both agile and scalable under intensifying demands.

STREAMLINING DATA RETRIEVAL

A large part of an app's responsiveness depends on how efficiently it handles data. Even if an application has a sleek user interface, over-fetching tables or retrieving unnecessary columns can inflate load times and sync durations. Prioritizing lean data retrieval is a cornerstone of superior performance.

- **Use Targeted Columns** – Restrict the columns your app downloads to what users truly need. This can be achieved by removing obsolete fields or creating narrower tables that focus on key attributes for the workflow at hand.
- **Limit Rows with Slices** – When handling large tables, define slices that filter out unneeded records for each user group. This approach significantly lightens data payloads during sync.
- **Implement Security Filters** – Beyond privacy advantages, security filters prevent non-essential data from even reaching the device, trimming synchronization processing and reducing bandwidth usage.

OPTIMIZING EXPRESSIONS AND CALCULATIONS

Expressions that run excessively or carry out unneeded calculations can degrade performance over time. By tailoring your logic for efficiency, you keep computations streamlined and avoid bottlenecks.

- **Consolidate Complex Logic** – Rather than scattering multiple conditional or lookup expressions in one formula, split them into smaller, well-named virtual columns. This eases debugging and can enhance recalculation speeds.
- **Cache Repetitive Lookups** – If you repeatedly reference the same data or relationships, store these outcomes in a virtual column. Trimming repeated computations significantly lightens the load on sync routines.
- **Precompute Worthy Summaries** – For heavy aggregations (e.g., monthly sales totals, advanced metrics), consider saving partial or final results in a dedicated table or column. This prevents real-time reprocessing each time a user opens the app.

REFINING WORKFLOWS AND AUTOMATIONS

Complex workflows and Bots can put strain on your app's performance if they're triggered unnecessarily or contain redundant steps. A well-tuned automation layer keeps everything running smoothly without sapping responsiveness.

- **Reduce Redundant Actions** – If multiple actions are essentially duplicating tasks, consolidate them. Each unneeded workflow step adds overhead and can slow the user experience.
- **Adopt Event-Driven Timing** – Allow triggers to fire only when required fields change or certain conditions appear, as opposed to running them every time a row is edited in unrelated columns.
- **Schedule Non-Urgent Tasks** – Bots that handle bulk processing or periodic checks might run after business hours or at spaced intervals. This approach ensures your

daytime operations remain unimpeded by large-scale tasks.

EMBRACING DATABASE EFFICIENCIES

Beyond AppSheet's own optimizations, judicious use of your underlying data source can amplify performance gains. When the database is properly structured and indexed, queries become more efficient.

- **Index Key Columns** – Help your database respond rapidly to queries by indexing columns frequently used for filtering or linking (e.g., reference keys).
- **Partition High-Volume Tables** – Splitting huge tables by date, region, or other logical boundaries can reduce query scope, improving read and write speeds.
- **Monitor Transaction Loads** – In fast-changing environments, excessive concurrent writes can stall performance. If needed, batch updates or adopt row-level locking strategies to avoid contention.

BALANCING REAL-TIME NEEDS WITH SYNC INTERVALS

Not every bit of data must update instantaneously. Deciding which elements truly require real-time refreshes and which can follow a slower schedule ensures that sync times are kept under control.

- **Staggered Refresh Cycles** – High-priority info (e.g., live order statuses) might auto-sync frequently, whereas archival or reference data can update less often to reduce system load.

- **User-Initiated Syncs** – For certain tasks, prompt the user to sync only when they need the latest data. This approach grants autonomy over timing and further conserves resources.
- **Incremental vs. Full Sync** – When possible, configure incremental syncs that transfer only changed or new records, minimizing overhead for returning users.

TESTING AND ONGOING PERFORMANCE MONITORING

Optimizing performance isn't a one-off endeavor. Constant monitoring and iterative testing confirm that fine-tuning efforts remain effective as your app scales or acquires new features.

- **Leverage Performance Profiling** – AppSheet's performance tools provide insight into sync durations, expression execution times, and overall data transfer volumes.
- **Conduct Stress Tests** – Before major rollouts, simulate peak loads by increasing test user counts or bulk updating data. Look for early clues of bottlenecks or slowdowns.
- **Review Incrementally** – Each time you introduce a new table, workflow, or expression, revisit your performance metrics. Quick interventions help sidestep cumulative drag later.

CONCLUSION

Cultivating high-performance AppSheet solutions demands an ongoing focus on efficiency. By trimming data retrieval, streamlining expressions, optimizing automations, and harnessing scalable database practices, you ensure your application remains nimble—even as requirements expand. These best practices, combined with real-time monitoring and periodic performance evaluations, form the foundation for apps that not only fulfill business goals but deliver swift, engaging user experiences.

Chapter 22: Machine Learning and Predictive Insights in AppSheet

Harnessing machine learning (ML) and predictive insights can transform your AppSheet applications from simple data trackers into forward-looking assets that anticipate user needs and deliver proactive intelligence. By identifying hidden patterns, forecasting future trends, and offering personalized suggestions, ML capabilities help enterprises achieve outcomes that span improved customer engagement, operational efficiency, and strategic planning. In this chapter, we'll explore strategies for integrating predictive models and automations into your AppSheet workflows, along with recommendations to keep these models both relevant and responsible.

SCOPING AND PREPARING DATA FOR ML

At the core of every machine learning endeavor lies high-quality data. Before introducing ML, assess the types of questions your teams want answered—such as predicting sales cycles, pinpointing equipment downtime, or identifying anomalies in expense reports. Next, ensure your data columns and relationships align with those objectives:

- **Comprehensive Yet Focused Datasets** – Strike a balance by including fields that directly influence predictive accuracy without cluttering your model with irrelevant details.
- **Clean and Consistent Inputs** – Standardize key variables like dates, categories, and numerical ranges to provide a stable foundation for forecasting or classification. Address missing values thoughtfully, whether by imputation or removing partial records that threaten model integrity.
- **Representative Historical Records** – For time-based analyses (e.g., predicting product demand), ensure your table spans enough past data to capture seasonal or cyclical trends that shape your predictions.

SELECTING ML SERVICES AND INTEGRATION PATHS

While AppSheet doesn't natively train full-fledged models within the platform, you can connect to external services for everything from data enrichment to running predictions. Several approaches stand out:

- **Built-In AI Features** – Ever-evolving AppSheet intelligence might include features that suggest automated workflows or column constraints based on usage patterns. Stay tuned for updates that simplify predictive tasks directly within the editor.
- **Cloud AI APIs** – Tools like Google Cloud's AutoML or public REST APIs can generate predictions from your AppSheet data. You can structure a Bot that calls an API endpoint, passes relevant row information, and updates a column with the predicted outcome.
- **Custom Script Bridges** – If your organization employs data scientists, embed their advanced ML models via

Apps Script or external connectors. Predictions produced externally can be injected back into your AppSheet tables, ensuring a seamless user experience.

AUTOMATING PREDICTIONS WITHIN WORKFLOWS

Predictions are most impactful when integrated into daily operations. By weaving them into AppSheet workflows, you offer timely insights to decision-makers or even automate responses to emerging trends:

- **Trigger-Based Forecasting** – Whenever a new record is added or updated, a Bot can invoke a model with the latest inputs, returning an up-to-date forecast. This ensures smooth synchronization between data entry and predictive outputs.
- **Automated Alerts** – When predicted outcomes surpass predefined thresholds—such as a high churn risk—your application can alert specific teams via SMS, email, or chat, prompting immediate intervention.
- **Ranked Recommendations** – Create a list of recommended actions (e.g., top products to restock, customers to follow up with) based on predictive scores. Display these ranked suggestions in a custom dashboard, helping users tackle priority items first.

MAINTAINING MODEL ACCURACY OVER TIME

Machine learning models require continuous health checks. As your business evolves, data patterns change, causing predictive accuracy to drift. Ensure your AppSheet-based solutions remain relevant by:

- **Regular Retraining** – If external systems build your models, schedule periodic retraining using the latest data. Align these cycles with significant shifts—like product launches or seasonal transitions—to capture new trends effectively.
- **Split Test Approaches** – Compare new model versions against older baselines with partial user groups or shadow testing. For example, run two variations of a predictive module side by side and evaluate which yields better real-world results.
- **Feedback Loops** – Encourage end-users to report incorrect or unexpected recommendations directly in the app. These user insights can guide data scientists or algorithm owners in refining future iterations.

ETHICAL AND RESPONSIBLE AI USAGE

Predictive solutions can improve decisions, but they must be applied responsibly. Safeguard users, customers, and partners by considering licit and ethical dimensions:

- **Data Privacy and Security** – Ensure that only approved roles can view sensitive columns used in modeling. If you share data with external ML systems, confirm compliance with relevant regulations.
- **Bias Monitoring** – A model trained on unrepresentative data may produce skewed outcomes. Periodically test results across demographics or categories to detect potential biases and adjust training sets accordingly.
- **Transparent Explanations** – Offer high-level rationale behind recommendations. Simplified "reason codes" help downstream users trust your predictions and pinpoint anomalies.

VISUALIZING PREDICTIONS AND INSIGHTS IN APPSHEET

Predictions gain traction when users can interpret forecasts at a glance. With AppSheet, you have multiple avenues for presenting insights in an interactive, actionable format:

- **Charts with Predicted Trends** – Overlay forecast lines on existing metrics, enabling quick comparisons of actual vs. expected performance. Color-coded thresholds highlight risk levels or deviation that demands scrutiny.
- **Aggregated Scoreboards** – Summarize predictions (e.g., churn probability) in top-level KPI cards. A daily or weekly scoreboard fosters immediate awareness and helps teams prioritize follow-ups.
- **Interactive Drill-Down** – When users click a predicted value, configure a deep link to the underlying data or a detail view explaining how that forecast was derived. This context cements trust and understanding.

CONCLUSION

Machine learning and predictive insights can elevate ordinary data-driven apps into powerful enablers of strategic foresight. By combining robust data preparation, well-chosen external ML services, and streamlined user workflows, you empower teams to act swiftly on predicted outcomes. Monitoring model performance—and remaining vigilant about fairness, privacy, and transparency—helps maintain an ethical, effective solution. In the end, these integrations not only enrich operational decision-making but also set the stage for future innovations, allowing your AppSheet project to keep pace with dynamic market demands.

Chapter 23: Advanced Customization with App Scripts

AppSheet's powerful no-code platform inherently delivers robust functionality. However, there are times when you need even more specialized behavior—behaviors that aren't always attainable through standard expressions or built-in automation. In these scenarios, Google Apps Script can be your key to advanced customization. By linking additional scripts to your AppSheet app, you can harness the flexibility of custom functions, external data manipulation, and intricate process orchestration. This chapter explores methods for extending AppSheet's core capabilities with Apps Script, revealing how these two platforms can work in harmony to satisfy complex requirements.

ESTABLISHING THE APPS SCRIPT INTEGRATION

Before diving into sophisticated scripting, you must lay the groundwork by linking your Apps Script project to your AppSheet environment. Typically, this involves hosting your script in Google Workspace and granting the necessary permissions. Once connected, you can call upon your Apps Script resources through AppSheet automations or direct function calls.

Whether you aim to integrate an intricate business rule, connect to an external service, or process spreadsheet data with fine-grained logic, confirming that your script is properly authorized is critical. Keep track of script IDs, project credentials, and user-level permissions to ensure that your solution stays both functional and secure.

CREATING CUSTOM FUNCTIONS AND SERVICES

One of the major advantages of Apps Script is its ability to define custom functions that run server-side logic. These functions can handle tasks that exceed the scope of typical AppSheet expressions:

- **Data Cleanup** – Implement specialized routines to detect and fix irregular data patterns, such as merging nearly identical entries or adjusting inconsistent date formats before they reach your main AppSheet tables.
- **API Wrappers** – Build a thin layer on top of external APIs to simplify requests and responses. AppSheet automations can invoke these wrapper functions, rather than dealing with raw headers and payload parsing.
- **Advanced Validation** – If standard validation rule sets aren't sufficient, Apps Script functions can apply context-aware checks. For instance, verifying time availability based on advanced calendars or resource constraints beyond simple referencing.

TIMING AND TRIGGER STRATEGY

In many workflows, you may want script-based processes to run either on a set schedule or in response to specific events. While AppSheet's built-in Bots can handle core triggers, Apps Script offers added options such as:

- **Timer-Driven Triggers** – Schedule Apps Script functions to run daily, weekly, or at custom intervals. This approach can automate tasks like data archiving or large-scale reformatting without manual approval.
- **Spreadsheet Event Triggers** – If your app relies heavily on spreadsheets, you can connect to events such as form submissions or cell edits. Apps Script can immediately process the change, then reflect the outcome in AppSheet.
- **Post-Processing after AppSheet Actions** – Combine standard AppSheet actions with subsequent script calls for deeper follow-ups. For example, when a user finalizes a record, your script might generate a complex summary report and email it automatically to stakeholders.

EXPANDING WITH EXTERNAL INTEGRATIONS

Apps Script also shines when bridging AppSheet with external services and platforms. By configuring custom calls, you can weave data from across your ecosystem into AppSheet's front-end experience:

- **Synchronizing CRM Data** – If your organization stores leads in various external systems, a script can pull accounts and contact details into a consolidated AppSheet table. This ensures all relevant updates flow seamlessly in both directions.
- **Generating Custom Documents** – With script-based logic, you can merge AppSheet data into advanced document templates—like proposals or contracts—before distributing them electronically. Include brand-specific formatting, advanced calculations, or dynamic sections for a polished final output.
- **Notifications Across Platforms** – Apps Script can reach beyond standard email or SMS by messaging custom channels (such as Slack, Teams, or internal chat

systems). Your AppSheet triggers become the launchpad for sophisticated cross-platform alerts.

MANAGING SCRIPT PERFORMANCE AND EFFICIENCY

As you augment your application with powerful script routines, keep performance in mind. Overly complex calculations or frequent external calls can impede responsiveness if not planned carefully. A few essential considerations include:

- **Modular Code Organization** – Split large scripts into smaller, focused functions. This practice improves maintainability and fosters code reusability. Other developers can more quickly grasp your design, or adapt parts for new requirements.
- **Batch Processing** – If you must handle massive data sets, gather records in sizable chunks rather than line-by-line processing. This lowers overhead from repeated function calls and typically improves overall execution speed.
- **Usage Limits and Quotas** – Google Apps Script has daily quotas and rate limits. Ensure your design remains mindful of these constraints, especially if your enterprise solutions run processes at high volume.

IMPLEMENTING SECURITY BEST PRACTICES

When you integrate Apps Script with AppSheet, you introduce another layer of potential vulnerabilities. Prioritizing security fosters trust with users and protects sensitive information:

- **Principle of Least Privilege** – Restrict script access to only the data and services it truly needs. Excessive permissions broaden your risk surface.
- **Secure Storage of Credentials** – If your script interacts with external systems using private tokens or API keys, store them securely. Avoid embedding secrets in plain text. Instead, consider using utility classes or secure variables when possible.
- **Controlled Deployment** – Use versioning and thorough testing before deploying new or updated scripts. Oversee who can edit and publish these scripts to preserve integrity within your environment.

CONCLUSION

Advanced customization with Apps Script empowers you to transcend the inherent boundaries of a no-code environment, all while preserving the user-friendly nature of AppSheet. When deployed thoughtfully, scripts can orchestrate complex tasks, link external systems, and provide specialized logic that elevates your application's overall utility. By aligning robust security measures, organized code practices, and efficient data handling, you'll craft a seamless extension of AppSheet—where imaginative, script-driven enhancements solve unique enterprise challenges without sacrificing reliability or manageability.

Chapter 24: Leveraging AppSheet's Extensions and Add-ons

AppSheet's flexibility expands well beyond its core functionality when you incorporate various extensions and add-ons. These supplementary tools introduce specialized capabilities, integrate with broader ecosystems, and streamline tasks that might otherwise require significant manual effort. By tapping into official or community-driven extensions, you can create a robust set of features tailored to your exact objectives—whether that means automating specialized document workflows or connecting with enterprise-grade platforms for advanced data analysis.

EXPLORING THE LANDSCAPE OF APPSHEET EXTENSIONS

Extensions vary in purpose and complexity, from preconfigured connectors that link to popular data environments to specialized modules that enrich your interface. Here's how to make the most of them:

- **Verified Marketplace Add-Ons** – AppSheet's ecosystem includes vetted tools compatible across industries. These add-ons typically undergo testing to align with security standards, making them a reliable solution for immediate use.
- **Custom Engineered Plugins** – If you require a niche functionality, third-party developers can craft a custom extension. This targeted approach ensures your app supports unique workflows or integrates tightly with proprietary systems.
- **Open-Source Offerings** – Browse community-driven repositories for shared scripts or integrations. While these often require adapting, they can quickly kickstart your customization efforts.

SYNCHRONIZING WITH PRODUCTIVITY SUITES

Extensions often bridge AppSheet's app-building environment with productivity platforms like Google Workspace or Microsoft 365. When utilized intelligently, these integrations reduce redundant data entry and unite teams under consistent processes:

- **Accelerated Document Generation** – Linked add-ons can pull records from AppSheet and insert them into specially formatted Docs or Sheets for detailed reporting, invoicing, or project briefs.
- **Calendar and Scheduling Enhancements** – Extensions that synchronize time-driven records with a corporate calendar help teams coordinate events, reminders, and tasks from a single, familiar interface.
- **Cross-Platform Collaboration** – By connecting your app to shared workspaces, comments and updates made in spreadsheets or presentations reflect in real time within AppSheet, minimizing version conflicts.

AUTOMATING SPECIALIZED WORKFLOWS

Some add-ons exist specifically to handle complex tasks so you don't have to create them from scratch. They can automate specialized workflows, letting your teams focus on core objectives rather than repetitive chores:

- **Advanced PDF Processors** – If your organization deals with contracts or compliance documents, add-ons that merge dynamic data into templated PDFs—complete with e-sign capabilities—can dramatically cut down manual editing.

- **Inventory or Asset Monitors** – Integrations with IoT dashboards or logistic services allow real-time updates on stock levels or shipments, translating raw device data into clear insights within your AppSheet app.
- **Industry-Specific Modules** – Extensions tailored to healthcare, finance, or energy management bring purpose-built features like advanced scheduling algorithms, cost estimators, or compliance checks without forcing you to reinvent established best practices.

EVALUATING RISK AND SECURITY

While extensions amplify functionality, they also require diligent oversight. Always verify the trustworthiness of any add-on, particularly if it handles critical data or has broad app access. Keep these safeguards in mind:

- **Check Permissions Thoroughly** – An extension requesting all-table read/write access might be overreaching if it only needs partial data. Maintaining principle of least privilege helps protect sensitive information.
- **Review Extension Updates** – As vendors update their tools, watch release notes for changes in data flows or additional scopes. Reconduct security reviews if the extension's functionality shifts significantly.
- **Align with Organizational Policies** – If you work within regulated fields, incorporate each add-on into official compliance checks. Require sign-off from data governance or IT teams to confirm adherence to internal standards.

FOSTERING CUSTOM EXTENSION DEVELOPMENT

Commercially available add-ons may not always address every nuanced requirement within your processes. In such cases, guiding an internal or external developer to build a targeted solution can yield lasting benefits:

- **Collaborative Specs** – Draft precise needs, including data structures, event triggers, and anticipated user interfaces. Clarity reduces the risk of misaligned final products.
- **Iterative Piloting** – Begin with a proof-of-concept to validate the extension's core mechanics before layering on complex elements. Early testers supply practical feedback, ensuring a user-focused outcome.
- **Maintenance Strategy** – Confirm who will maintain the add-on post-deployment. Scheduling version reviews and periodic improvements keeps the extension relevant amid changing business climates.

CONCLUSION

By smartly leveraging AppSheet's extensions and add-ons, you enrich your application with sophisticated features that complement and elevate core functionalities. Whether integrating standard productivity workflows or adopting specialized solutions, each extension can tailor the user experience to match precise operational flows. Thoroughly evaluating security considerations and charting a roadmap for ongoing maintenance ensures these enhancements remain robust and dependable. In turn, a well-curated ecosystem of add-ons helps your AppSheet application continue meeting evolving demands without burdening teams with reinventing established solutions.

www.ingramcontent.com/pod-product-compliance
Lightning Source LLC
LaVergne TN
LVHW051243050326
832903LV00028B/2540